SPARE CHANGE

A true account of profound love, devastating loss, and one woman's journey to accept the unfathomable.

Bonnie Henriksen

Copyright © 2017 by Bonnie Henriksen.

All rights reserved. No part of this book may be reproduced in any written, electronic, recording, or photocopying without written permission of the publisher or author. The exception would be in the case of brief quotations embodied in articles or reviews and pages where permission is specifically granted by the publisher or author.

Bonnie Henriksen/Spare Change
Printed in the United States of America

Although every precaution has been taken to verify the accuracy of the information contained herein, the author and publisher assume no responsibility for any errors or omissions. No liability is assumed for damages that may result from the use of information contained within.
Spare Change/ Bonnie Henriksen -- 1st ed.

Contents

Introduction 1

Chapter 1 Happy Endings and a Broken Straw 3

Chapter 2 Giant Red Letters 49

Chapter 3 A Hurricane's Eye 65

Chapter 4 The Worst Best Note 77

Chapter 5 Two Little Words 119

Chapter 6 Pennies From Heaven 135

To Gabe, my sunshine forever. Your bravery, nonconformity and ability to love without measure has taught me who I want to be.

I wrote this book because I needed to read it 25 years ago. To the woman out there who is the younger version of me, this is for you. You are stronger than you feel.

Acknowledgements

It would have been an impossible task to finish this project without the unwavering support of certain people.

To Ben, Luke, Jordan, Martha and Anne, thank you for your unending encouragement and love. As difficult as some of the memories are, you pushed me to share them, believing that someone somewhere would find strength in my times of weakness. Thank you. I hope you are right.

To my fellow teachers and school administrators, thank you for giving me the time and space I needed to finish this once and for all. Your quiet support was heard loud and clear.

To Frank, thank you for having my back.

To Corey, thank you for knowing how to ask all the right questions. When I hit the wall and could write no more, you appeared and broke that wall down.

And to Gabe, for pushing me non stop to just finish the damn book, I heard you. Thank you Honey.

Introduction

Reflection is a powerful tool; painful at times but necessary for growth. Deciding to share my story so that future generations will not repeat my mistakes fuels the vessel that carries my persistence.

My story begged me to tell it. I didn't want to pen the episodes of my life; they were painful, and who was I to think I could write a book? But the story kept me up nights. It nagged at me that I couldn't lecture my sons and my fourth-grade students about taking risks and working hard unless I was willing to do the same. I had to share this story to be free of its weight.

I have taken a one-year leave of absence from my teaching position and moved into a tiny, distraction-free house with no cable and no Wi-Fi, determined to finish this project so that I can be the example I try to set for my kids. I bartend a few nights a week to pay the bills I do have, sustaining myself on free meals from the bar, and referred to by my friends as a pioneer girl because of the lifestyle I have adopted in order to finish this story.

Chapter 1

Happy Endings and a Broken Straw

I – July 1990

My name is Bonnie. I grew up the youngest of three girls in a middle-class subdivision in Fort Wayne, Indiana. My parents were loving and kind. I know my mom had the best intentions and did everything she could to help my two sisters and me be productive humans and good girls, but when asked to introduce us to people, she would always say, "This is Karen. She's the smart one. This is Laura. She's the talented one. And this is Bonnie. She's the cute one."

That emphasis on appearance would, unfortunately, impact the rest of my life.

Just like most girls do, I dreamed as a child that I'd grow up and marry a man who loved me and together, we'd build a family and walk off into the sunset. I've seen a few couples who have managed to succeed at that, but in reality, most people quickly realize that marriage is a whole lot of work—especially when you marry the wrong person.

After college graduation, I got my first teaching job in a small town in rural Georgia. I met my future husband shortly after I moved there, and quickly fell in love with the man I thought was perfect for me. In fact, I decided the first night I met Chad that I was going to marry him. He approached me in a piano bar and asked if he could take my picture. When I learned the camera didn't even have film in it, I was charmed at his feeble attempts to pick me up. We quickly began spending most of our weekends together, and after dating for a little over a year, he asked me to marry him.

Three days before the wedding that we had planned with full financing by my parents, my mom told me that I could cancel if I wanted to. She expressed concerns about his demeanor, stating that she thought he was going to be very domineering over me. The more she spoke, the more determined I was to make it work. I heard my mom's concerns and used them as fuel to justify my choice in a mate. Yes, he had some anger issues and yes, he seemed to be fueled by confrontation, but I believed these things could work themselves out because hey, he asked me to be his wife. He must love me, I thought.

Chad and I were married in July of 1990. We moved to Milwaukee, his home town, and I began teaching school while he used his VA benefits from his time in the Marine Corps to go to college. Our first son was born a year later and the other three would come in the following six years.

By all appearances, it would seem we were living the dream. The boys were my joy. They were healthy and kind and played like boys do, building forts and playing ball and eating lunches at the park. I was able to volunteer at school and cart them around to their sporting and school events, while Chad made a good income in his landscaping business with just enough administrative help from me. When we went places, everyone would see a smiling couple and I'm certain they would think, "What an adorable family."

"If only they knew what happens behind closed doors," I would think to myself.

Our first years were spent raising babies and trying to make ends meet, with occasional camping trips and lots of fights with make-up sex. I knew Chad had a wandering eye, and often felt a tinge of jealousy as he smiled at younger women with bodies that didn't have the battle scars of childbirth, but I tried to resolve those feelings—I was the one going home with him, making him breakfast and sleeping in his bed. He was passionate. He was driven. He openly stated many times to me that he would never repeat the mistakes his own dad made with regard to his marriage or raising children. I, naïve and cute, believed him.

When he told me a few days after our oldest son was born that I looked like a sack of potatoes, I believed him.

When he told me during an argument that I was a waste of human sperm, I believed him.

When I began to notice tabs open on the computer for porn sites and history searches on sites like "friend finder," I would ask him if I should be concerned and his answer was always no. When a woman called asking for Chad and I asked, "Who is this?" and she responded with, "Who is

THIS?" and I told her it was his wife, she hung up. When I asked him about it he successfully convinced me he had no clue who it could have been.

As a school kid, lined up to pick teams for kickball, I was always picked last. I was uncoordinated, nonathletic and chubby. I guess the easiest way to explain my mindset during the duration of the first fifteen years of my marriage is that Chad made me feel like I was still standing in that kickball line, waiting to be picked. I didn't know better at the time, so I found ways to justify his behavior and vowed to myself that I needed to keep working on me. I inferred that his wandering eye must reflect my inability to attract him and that anytime he got angry, it must have been because I failed to do something right.

While we didn't have a great marriage, I do have some happy memories. One year for Christmas he had a piano delivered to our house. I used it to play and for years I gave lessons to Gabe and Jordan. When the older boys were in Cub Scouts, Chad became a pack leader and spent a lot of energy putting together events for the kids. When my mom was dying, he drove me down to see her many times during that last year. There was just enough hope to keep me hanging on.

And hang on I did, pretending to the whole world that we were healthy and happy, wondering behind our closed doors if I would ever be enough of a woman to make him happy, internalizing his words and becoming more dependent on those brief moments of hope to keep any spark that remained, glowing.

II – March 2003

As tensions in the Gulf grew higher after the 9/11 attacks, war was imminent. Chad had joined the Army National Guard shortly after we were married, and was called to active duty in March of 2003. As his unit prepared for deployment, there was a family get-together at the armory on the day they were to leave for their training. We were told at that time that he would be gone at least six months. As the Hummers rolled out of the parking lot from the armory in Milwaukee, the boys stood on the curb and saluted every single one of them as they passed by.

One night in early May, while the boys and I were in Madison visiting my sister, he called. He told me that his commander had given them the night off and told them to call their wives and get together with them. I took this as a sign that he would be leaving the states soon, and I eagerly drove up to Tomah. We spent the night talking and making love in an old motel, and in the morning we kissed goodbye. We both knew we wouldn't see each other for a long time.

He left for Baghdad at the beginning of June.

All the boys knew about the war, and understood why he had to go and the dangers he would face. We reminisced often about happy memories we had, but for the most part, the boys carried on with life as normal. At ages 12 and 10, Ben and Luke became the men of the family, helping me with Gabe and Jordan. Frequently, I'd wake up in the morning to one or more boys in my bed. I watched the news in private, not wanting to scare the kids with the reports of all the fighting that was going on, but I didn't lie to them about what their dad was doing. They knew he was in the Green Zone, they knew he carried a loaded gun, and when a female soldier from his unit was killed, they knew.

We lived at the end of a cul-de-sac. We were told that if something ever happened to Chad, we would be notified in person. Living in a small town and on a very quiet road, it became a habit to stop what we were doing and hold our breath for a moment when an unknown car drove down the street. We all secretly hoped it wouldn't pull into our driveway. Looking back, I can almost remember the emotions associated with much of his time at war. I can also remember the atmosphere at home.

During his time away, we grew. The boys got bigger, stronger and smarter. They carried on, and the older two stepped up and helped me care for Gabe and Jordan as well as helping more around the house. I lost weight and gained confidence in myself as I carried on the business, paid the bills, and managed to keep the boys healthy and on the right track. We made movies and sent them to Chad, and he was able to call and e-mail on occasion. Most of what he told me was about the living and working conditions in Iraq. He would ask for packages with things like paper clips and notes from the boys. He would talk about the bureaucracies of Army life, the crappy food, and how much he missed us. I would read and reread his e-mails for days, until the next one came. He sent letters to each of the boys, telling them how proud he was of them, reminding them to help me, and encouraging them to keep doing well in school.

It seemed to me during that time that our relationship was becoming tighter. Reading his words of his love for me and the boys gave me energy for the work I was doing here. Living in the small town meant that everyone knew our situation and people were eager to help however they could. The sentiments Chad showed when he knew he had a community of support expressed gratitude and joy at how loved we really were. From a distance, my husband appeared to be softening; I felt refreshed and for the first time in years, hopeful.

Hopeful, yet still a realist. Our community has an indoor aquatic center that is open year-round. One dreary day in November, I took the boys there to get some exercise and have a needed break from the monotony of the needs of the business. While swimming, I banged my left hand against the wall of the pool and two diamonds from my wedding band broke off. I frantically dove under the water to retrieve them, successfully, but then felt a surge of despair and worry... "Broken ring, broken marriage?" was all I could think about for the next several days. At the time, I kept telling myself to stop over-analyzing it, but I couldn't help it...it just seemed like an omen and it truly scared me, to the point of e-mailing Chad and asking him if I should be worried. His answer was, of course, no. So I put the diamonds in my jewelry box and wore that broken ring. Every time I looked at it, though, I wondered; there was no reassurance in my head or heart that my marriage wasn't very broken.

He was given a two-week leave of absence at Christmas. The day he flew into Milwaukee, I put on a pretty dress, pulled the boys out of school, and we eagerly drove to the airport to greet him. Walking down the hall, it was heartwarming to see him crouch down and hug them, then move in to give me a great big hug. We didn't have a lot of time, but I was very excited that he was home for the holidays, and in my mind, I was hopeful we would make great memories.

I noticed that first night that his pelvic area was shaved. He never did that before, and it caused me to pause and wonder. We made love anyway. The next morning, I went to the office and noticed that he was e-mailing a woman by the name of Jessie, from his unit. His explanation was that he needed to tell her not to bother him for two weeks. I'm not sure why I believed that, since looking back now that pretty much told the story, but I did. He mentioned her name a few more times and then proceeded to tell me that they had become good friends, and were spending so much time together that the unit commander asked him if they were having an affair. His answer, of course, was no.

He left to go back to Iraq right after New Year's and wouldn't come home again until July, when his unit's time was up. Our routine continued as it had before his break, and in July, we were all ecstatic at the prospect of him coming home for good.

In early July, we were notified that his unit's plans for departure were finalized, and that week the entire Company left Baghdad and flew to Kuwait to pack up and prepare for the return home.

The day that his plane was scheduled to arrive, the boys and I got dressed up, bought flowers, made a poster, and got in the car for the happiest ride ever. Waiting at the hangar at Douglas Field, chatting with the other wives and kids, an announcement came over the loudspeaker to look up at the sky. The plane was preparing to land. The feeling that I had, watching this plane, knowing he was in it, safe and healthy, made me overcome with emotions of joy, relief and happiness. Getting off the plane, he was greeted with cheers, smiles, and lots of hugs. Seeing him took my breath away. Knowing he was alive, he was coming home, we could be a family again, had me walking on clouds. He kissed me passionately and we spent the afternoon giving interviews to the press with our arms wrapped around each other. I can say that was easily one of the happiest days of our marriage.

He had to stay at Fort McCoy for a few days for medical tests and a time of decompression. We went back up to get him on July 28, our 14-year anniversary. We were required to go to meetings to help us understand the symptoms of PTSD as well as tips for us to help make a smooth transition back to normalcy. He introduced me to Jessie that day, explaining that she was his friend, and we shook hands and smiled genuinely at each other. She was a tall woman, not attractive by his standards, and married with two young children. I remember not feeling anything about meeting her; this woman he had spoken of must have just been a great friend, and I was honestly happy that he found someone to talk to, as friends had always been difficult for him to keep.

Two days after he was home, his brother and family came over for a cookout and some beach time, including riding our jet ski. While he was gone, the boys and I had not ridden it at all, and upon trying to start it up, he realized the battery was dead. He asked why I hadn't changed it, and began yelling at me in front of the boys and his brother, asking how hard could it have been to change a battery so he could come home from serving his country and enjoy a ride. He then went into the garage to look for a charger. He called me in there and began yelling that the garage was messy. He couldn't understand how I let it get so bad, and expressed his disgust at my obvious laziness.

I began to cry.

He then yelled about that, asking me why I was crying, when he was the one who just served 444 days for his country. I recall standing there wondering how I could have been so foolish, to think he had changed…

As his presence became known in the community, a lot of well-meaning visitors stopped by with gifts. He loved talking about his time overseas, and people were full of gratitude for him. It was very sweet, and as I watched and listened, he even had me convinced that he must've been the most important soldier in his unit. The pride I felt at the fact that my husband had served for all of us etched its way into my heart, while I quickly reverted back to my old ways of defending his arrogant and rude nature. It took only a matter of a few days to begin losing myself again, after all the growth I had done. My sisters noticed it pretty quickly and mentioned it to me, but I would hear nothing of it...all the kudos Chad was getting were well deserved.

III - **August 2004**

We took the kids to Orlando for a long vacation a few weeks after his return.

One day, at Universal Studios, a woman mentioned to Chad that he was smoking in a non-smoking area of the park. He responded, "I just got back from serving your country for 444 days in Iraq. I'll smoke wherever I want to."

She didn't like his answer and she dumped a large cup of soda on him. He then took his cigarette and put it on her shirt, then pushed her teenage daughter when she tried to stop the fight. Ben (our oldest son) was standing off to the side, screaming, "Mom! Stop them! Do something!"

I stood there in shock, scared to say anything, holding the three younger ones back from the chaos.

A security guard was called in and we were all taken to an office to give a deposition. I fluffed the story so that Chad wouldn't look so bad, and he walked away with a slap on the hand and a warning to tone himself down while at the park.

About a month after our return from Orlando, Chad and I took a trip together to Reno. The kids stayed with a friend of ours in Wisconsin.

Walking through a casino one night on the way to dinner, I had my arm in his. He stated that I was his "trophy wife." I didn't like the way that felt, yet I didn't say anything about it at the time. It caused me to wonder if he saw me for anything but my looks. It also reminded me of how my mom would introduce my sisters and me to new people. I grew up feeling like all I had to live up to was being cute. I hated the way that felt, and often found myself seeking validation that I was smart or talented like my sisters.

At a very high-class restaurant one night, we got to talking about Jessie (the girl from his unit in Iraq). I can't recall much of the conversation other than talking about her career and marriage, but I do remember asking him why he liked her so much, considering that she was full-time Army (and he always referred to women in the armed forces as a waste of money). He became extremely defensive, raising his voice, and while I tried to calm him down, he simply got up and left the restaurant. I scrambled through my purse to find some money to leave on the table and then scurried out to find him. We spent the next several hours in the hotel room arguing, until finally we had sex and carried on as usual. I remember at that moment just knowing that he had been sexual with her; the questions from his unit commander were validated, and all I wondered was how long it went on, how frequent their encounters were, and whether or not he loved her. I never told him how I felt. Instead, I pushed it to the back of my mind, telling myself that I was imagining things, but at the same time allowing that he probably had reason to have cheated…after all, he was in a war, for crying out loud! How would I know how that feels, waking up each morning and not knowing if I'm going to live through the day? I found a way to rationalize his probable behavior as though it was something he should've done to help him feel better.

After returning from our trip, the boys got settled into their routine at school (Jordan, the youngest, was in first grade at that point). I continued doing landscape design and the paperwork for the business, as well as being a homemaker and a volunteer at the kids' school. One day while Chad was home for lunch, his phone rang. When he picked up, I heard a woman on the other end who simply said "HI!" in a loud, excitable voice—the kind that shows how happy you are to hear someone's voice. We made eye contact at that point and while he engaged in small talk with her, I kept one ear open while I pretended to stay busy in the kitchen. Though I couldn't hear the details of what they were talking about, I could tell by his tone that he was excited to hear her too. When he hung up, I asked who it was, and he told me it was a customer. I guess by that point in time he figured I didn't have the courage to badger him into telling me the truth, so I let it go, knowing it was a girlfriend, and being, for some reason, complacent to that idea.

One day, he came home from work, and I was wearing a pair of tight jeans and a lacy shirt. Instead of telling me that I looked nice, he accused me of having an affair and getting dressed like that to gain attention from other men. I looked at him, speechless, because he could not have been more wrong. I had dressed up for him.

At one point shortly after that, he noticed that one of the bathroom toilets had a rust ring around the inside, and he called me into the bathroom, telling me to get some bleach

Happy Endings and a Broken Straw

and scrub it with my bare hands. The words he said to me have had lasting effects; I have never, since that day, used a toilet brush again. I guess there's some kind of gratifying self-punishment in the idea that I'm not worthy of using a brush.

It was like the louder he lived, the more quietly I did. I was suffocating and I didn't even know it; I was desensitized to love, normalcy, dreams, and sex. I had been reduced to mediocrity with tolerance for just about anything when it came to how I was treated, and even though I was crying inside, I tried not to let it show. I needed to keep our family whole, whatever the cost. Looking back now, I understand that I was too scared to leave.

For Christmas, we went to my dad's house in Indiana. My sister Laura was there with her husband and kids. As is our tradition on Christmas night, we played bingo. We always bought prizes from the dollar store and everyone who won got to pick a prize, separated into piles by kids and adults. Well, Laura's son Andrew got a "Bingo" and went to pick a prize. He wanted one from the adult pile, and we told him that was fine. Chad didn't like that, and proceeded to begin yelling at both Andrew and me in a very demeaning way. Andrew started to cry, and in my disgust at Chad's cruelty to the child and me, I simply put my jacket on and went outside for a long walk to cry it out. I remember being far from my dad's house when I heard Laura calling my name; she was worried. I came back later that night, packed up the boys' things, and we left for home early the next morning. My dad and sister hugged me and the kids, but no one said goodbye to Chad, and he didn't offer a word to anyone either.

My dad and my sister became completely aware during those days of just how awful things were in my marriage, but offered no suggestions of what to do. I believe that on some level, they may have thought he was suffering from PTSD; I never bought into that idea, simply because I was reminded time and again that this man was exactly the same as he had been through our entire marriage. I do recall my dad telling me over the phone, a couple of weeks later, that he knew how Chad would talk highly about me in front of others but treat me so horribly in the privacy of our home. That validation didn't make me feel any better. In fact, it may have been the vessel for me to begin acknowledging that my marriage was actually failing, and that others could see it too. I'm not sure what it was about allowing others to think I had a great marriage; I don't know if it was my own way of thinking "fake it till you make it" or if it was something I carried with me from childhood, regarding image and caring what others thought. Perhaps I needed to go along with the show so that I could continue trying to validate Chad's worth and importance, still believing somehow that he would become a better husband if I could just be a better wife.

There was an Army Christmas party that year in Madison. It was a formal event, held at a hotel. Upon arriving, I saw a few women I had met during the deployment. Jessie, Chad's friend, came up to me and said, in a condescending tone that I will never forget, "Well, hello, Miss Bonnie."

He forgot about my birthday that year. The day came and went with no mention by him, so I fixed dinner and mentioned while we ate that it was my birthday. He looked at me and said, "Well, Happy Fucking Birthday" right in front of the kids. I recall looking at each of my boys right then and having not a single word to say. My gaze fell to my lap as I worked hard to fight back the tears that wanted to come.

The drama, frustration, hurt, and walking on eggshells continued, until one night in June of 2005 when I went on the computer and logged into *Yahoo* mail. Somehow, Chad had his own e-mail account that I didn't know of, and he had left it open. Being curious, I scrolled through the messages, finding several to Jessie over the past year. I became instantly nauseous at the sight of the words they wrote to each other, talking about me, the boys, and their love for one another.

As awful as it sounds, I wished right then that he had died in Iraq so that he could have some honor attached to his name.

I printed the messages, turned off the computer, and brought the boys to a friend's house. I then showed all of the e-mails to Chad. He denied it at first, telling me it was a game. When I threatened to call Jessie, he confessed. He told me that they had a "marriage" of sorts that began in Kuwait before they even arrived in Iraq, shortly after he left home in March of 2003. He told me that she was referred to as his "wife" by other members of his unit. He described how they would spend nearly every waking hour together, and they had a special closet set up so that at night they could go have sex. He told me about some kind of a box he built for them to have sex on, and that he and Jessie would joke about how he said he would build one for him and me to use. He told me that each night, one or the other would go to the computer and print each other's e-mails. That part made me sick, thinking that I had written so many private, heartfelt letters to him, and that she had likely read every one of them. I sat there, speechless, while he spewed the details of their relationship in a manner that actually seemed a little like bragging. And there I was again, standing in that kickball line.

It was as though there was a third person in our marriage, someone I didn't invite but that Chad did, who knew everything about me but I knew nothing about her. It was sickening to me.

All the e-mails he had written to me and the boys, telling us how much he missed us; all the phone calls in the middle of the night, telling me how he yearned for me... I realized at that moment that it was all a lie. The truth was that he didn't allow time to miss us, didn't allow loneliness to grip his core, didn't consider those four adorable faces or his wife at home, awaiting his safe return. That's the part that hurt the most, and to this day, still does. We were insignificant.

For years before I began to discover the truth, I had suspicions that he was cheating. Early on, I expressed my concern to him but was told repeatedly to mind my own business and work on myself; his conditioning worked and I began to simply hold everything inside, rationalizing that if he was cheating, I must not be worthy of his exclusive attention.

Looking back now, I realize what a pussy I was. My husband bullied me and I let him.

During the first seven years of our marriage, I had four babies that obviously required a large part of my time and most of my energy. Between work, motherhood and homemaking, he was left with a run-down wife who also happened to acquire a "baby pouch" complete with stretch marks. My mom told me, shortly before we were married, that in order to have a successful marriage I needed to be a "lady in the kitchen and a whore in the bedroom." I struggled with the notion for years that I was failing at both, because the image I believed men saw as beautiful didn't have the mileage of what carrying a few babies does to a woman. I thought ladies look like June Cleaver, and whores certainly don't have stretch marks. Why I believed that fucked-up notion, I don't know. Why I thought he deserved some perfectly shaped, always serving, agreeable woman to bow to his every beck and call, I don't know. It's really all a bunch of shit and now I shudder at the idea that I believed any of it.

Looking back, I can't say that I would have even been able to do anything differently and honestly, I'm not sure that I would have wanted to. For years, I thought his infidelity was my fault. Chad repeatedly told me that if I were a better housewife, thinner, smarter, more adventurous in bed, blah blah freaking blah, he wouldn't have to look elsewhere. While that may be true, his inability to be faithful to his wife speaks nothing of me and everything about him. Either you are a loyal person or you are not...there's no in-between.

I also want to be clear on this: I don't hate Chad. I disagree with his behavior and I loathe his lack of self-control. But he is the father of my children, and I know he loves them in the best way he knows how. His own childhood was somewhat dysfunctional, and while that does not excuse his actions, I do have an understanding of the cycles we humans are unable (or unwilling) to stop. I like to think that he hopes and prays our children can stop the cycle; I am highly optimistic that they already have.

Despite the fact that I had imagined or probably known bits and pieces of his infidelity over the years, up to that point, I thought it was all physical. I'm not trying to dismiss his behavior or rationalize it being OK, I'm just saying that in my heart, I always knew I was the one cooking, caring for his kids, helping, planning, and waking up with him each day. The whole game changed the moment I realized she was his "wife." It was at that moment that I felt the surge of disgust at the idea that I was truly replaceable; I had no more value than the spare change a rich man throws to a beggar.

Chad and I began going to counseling once the cat was out of the bag, in an attempt to repair the marriage. If nothing else, I knew that if we wound up divorcing, I wanted to be able to tell my sons that I did everything I possibly could to save the marriage. We spent time mainly with our pastor, but also visited a couple of psychologists.

Chad's approach to counseling, on the outside, was that he was willing to do whatever it would take to keep his family whole and to try and prove his love for me. My approach was different—I was seeking a way to feel better, validation of my pain, and to learn whether we should keep trying or get divorced.

I cannot describe why, but I wanted details. I asked question after question for what seems like weeks. While I understand that placed him in a precarious position, Chad was advised by both the pastor and the psychologists that whatever I asked, he needed to answer truthfully.

Talking with him was like one interrogation after another. He'd sit there with a straight face and offer nothing; I had to come up with all the questions. What I wanted was for him to just spill his guts and tell me every single gory detail that he'd been hiding all those years, yet he made me work so hard just to get the little information he was willing to share. And even when he did give me answers, I never knew if he was telling the whole truth, a blatant lie, or just part of what actually happened. There were so many things he said to me that caused me to have more questions, many which caused me to question myself. When I asked him if he ever told her he loved her, he responded, "I can't recall." When I asked him if they had sex in Fort McCoy, he said, "There are lines I wouldn't cross." When I asked him when he had his first affair, he said, "This is about Jessie."

Sadly, I didn't realize how manipulative and insulting his answers were at the time; it is only now, looking back, that I understand the lengths he went to in giving me non-answers.

I tried to forgive him. I tried looking at him with new eyes. During the time that we sought counseling, I worked hard to learn that what he did doesn't define who he is. While I still believe that to be true, when I found him continuing to seek other women, looking at porn, and (for the most part) only telling me he loved me when we were having sex, forgiving became a constant battle. It was like the shit kept piling up on top of me and just when I had a chance to see the light, he'd throw more onto the pile.

One night, he asked me to put my finger someplace it really shouldn't have been. When he woke up bleeding the next day, he asked me why I assaulted him. He was serious, and I was scared out of my mind. I clearly remembered what had happened, yet I still questioned myself and my memory. I think at that moment I felt a sense of how dangerous the man I called my husband might actually be.

After about six months of discussions (interrogations), I learned that while he admitted to being with other women during our engagement, his first extramarital affair happened just a few weeks after our oldest son was born. Even though it was crippling in many ways, there was something very freeing to me about knowing what I was dealing with. This was a man who was never interested in, maybe not even capable of, being in a committed marriage.

Ben and Luke, at that time 14 and 12, made it very clear that they wanted us to work through this. I recall our pastor making this comment, after one particularly good session in which I thought Chad was showing remorse: "Well, look at this...here you have a mistreated, overworked, underappreciated, cheated-on wife with the potential to have a marriage happier than you could ever imagine."

That gave me just enough motivation to keep working at it.

Earlier in 2005, before I found out about Jessie, we made the decision that our family had outgrown the home we were living in. We found a six-acre parcel of land for sale and bought it, hired an architect to design our dream home, and began the process of building it. Chad served as the general contractor, and immersed himself fully into the whole process while I simply offered opinions and showed up with food for him on occasion. During the summer months, when I found out about Jessie, work on the house slowed down, but he had vowed to finish it, even if that meant selling it right away.

IV – November 2005

I had always told Chad he was extreme. That is an astute way to describe his personality. He does everything in an extreme way, from hands-on projects to the way he states his opinions to his eating habits to his temper. Extreme. There is no "just kinda" in his existence, and on many levels, that is a good thing. People knew this about him and were completely turned off by it, scared by it, or highly attracted to it.

{24}

The house project got out of hand pretty quickly. My vision of living in a sturdy yet practical country home was quickly taken over by a 3,600-square foot home with a 6-car garage, 5 bedrooms and 3.5 baths. The kitchen had an island that was 16 feet long and could easily serve as a belly-up bar to at least 10 people. The insulation was sprayed, the siding was concrete board, the fireplace was 20 feet tall with a wood burner built in. The family room/kitchen area was below a loft that overlooked it all, and speaking in that house meant that unless you were in a bathroom with the door shut, you could hear your own echo. In building it, he added what is called a bonus room above the garage. At the time, we didn't know what it would be used for, but the price was right to add it, and he thought it would be a good addition. When designing, he asked me what I wanted. My requests were simple: a warm bedroom, laundry on the main floor, and a covered front porch with a porch swing. Though I didn't get the swing, he did provide for my other desires. My point is, it was the extreme house. Nothing was done half-assed, and I can remember him asking a friend to come over so he could give him a tour of his "mini mansion."

I realized during that first year after moving in just how far away from other people we were. The parcel of land was actually in the middle of several cornfields and we had few neighbors; town was nine miles away and a walk simply meant strolling along the edge of a road with nothing but farms to look at. I was beginning to feel secluded. I didn't like how that felt and mentioned it to Chad; his suggestion was that we have more parties. When I mentioned it to my dad, he told me that was all part of Chad's plan—to get me away from other people.

One night we were making love and he accidentally called me Jessie. I stopped, sat straight up, and said, "What did you call me?"

He said, "I said 'Jesus Christ.'" We both knew that was a lie. What happened that night changed the whole intimacy game for me; never again would I feel the satisfaction of feeling loved and cared for during sex with my own husband.

At that moment, when he said her name while I was lying naked with him, I realized that he was thinking about her. Knowing that, I became both desensitized and distant to the idea of making love; it would from then on just be sex.

The frequency didn't slow because of it, but I realized, about six months after it happened, that I was no longer present during the act of sex. To tolerate it, I learned how to pretend that I was one of the other women he had been with. I'd close my eyes and imagine that we were in whatever place they did it, and I was his mistress…in my mind, he was excited and aroused at whoever I was (because that's who he actually wanted to be with, I thought), and I was able to achieve orgasm almost every time because of the fact that I wasn't Bonnie.

This went on for seven years.

I told Chad about it a couple of times; he was upset and didn't like the idea, but neither of us knew what to do about it, so we simply continued our habits as though it was just a cross I had to bear. He did try to make things better; he would often apologize to me right in the middle of the act...when he sensed that I had phased out and wasn't really there, he'd simply say, "I'm so sorry." That never helped; in fact, it made me feel worse because he didn't apologize at any other times. To me, his apology was just an attempt to make sex better, which would benefit him, yet I still believed in some warped way that I needed to sustain the dysfunction or else he'd go find another mistress and I'd want to leave. That idea—leaving—was so far inside a box of "things that scare the shit out of me" that I continued submitting in that bed.

During the time of counseling with our pastor, our spirituality began to grow. It seemed to be the only hope we had for the idea that the marriage could possibly be saved. We would spend time as a family reading the Bible; we went to church every Sunday and were actively involved. Chad gave himself (with the prompting of our pastor) the title of the "Spiritual Leader of the Family." From the outside, pretty much everyone would see this as a good thing, and for quite a long time, I chose to believe that his newfound love of God was real, necessary, and quite possibly the biggest blessing I had ever received. After all, so much of the Bible talks about how to treat a wife and kids, how to live on the straight and narrow, and how to maintain pure relationships.

Something never felt quite right about it to me though, but I had a hard time putting my finger on it. Some mornings, I would wake up and find, sitting on the kitchen counter, an open Bible with a highlighted verse and a Post-it note that would say, "Bonnie read this—it's for you," or something similar to that. I always did as he told me, but whatever the message was inside the words, I don't think I ever quite got the literal meaning, simply because I was always scratching my head, wondering if his method of "leading" was even kind. I mean, I guess on the one hand, it's good that he was trying. But I had a difficult time wrapping my brain around the idea that he was finding verses for me; I guess I felt like since he was the one with the betrayal issues, he should be working on himself.

He also began to use God as a weapon. By that, I mean that in every argument or discussion we would have, he always found a way to quote a Bible verse to end the conversation. Don't get me wrong; I don't have an issue with people who argue using biblical references. But this was different. He took everything as so fundamentally literal within the Bible that once he found the "ace" he needed, he'd run with it, and there was nothing I could say to try to help him see my point of view. The irony in all of it, however, was the way he would justify his own behavior yet condemn the actions of others (especially me).

I began to question God's existence and what was even real; I couldn't understand how he was able to use scripture in his own favor but against me, and it all seemed very hypocritical. At the same time, he was becoming rather flamboyant about religion; he began to fast, he'd claim God spoke to him, and he researched how to speak in tongues.

The ripple effects of this new environment would leave a devastating effect on my spirituality.

Shortly before Christmas in 2006, I went on the computer one morning. Out of either old habit or curiosity (and possibly even by chance), I opened up the history. I found that Chad had been on a website viewing women who were modeling bikinis but with no tops on. My heart sank. I realized these pictures were tame compared to some of the things I'd seen him view in years past, but I was saddened and distraught that the man who seemed to be changing, and who now professed to having extreme views in the other direction about what it meant to be a real man, had apparently fallen backwards. When he came home, I asked him about it. He quickly replied that he wanted to buy me a swimsuit for Christmas and was looking, but accidentally came across those photos. I didn't believe him but I dropped the subject anyway.

Christmas came and went, and as my recollection of that holiday is weak, I assume it was fairly forgettable. However, our New Year's celebration left me with vivid memories.

Chad, though generally rather introverted and shy around groups of people, loved having get-togethers at our house. Some told me they thought it was a way for him to show off all of his possessions, but I actually believe he just loved the sights and sounds of people in his home, enjoying what he could offer them. We agreed on a party of mostly church folks to ring in the New Year, though I was reluctant to do so. I'd had experiences in getting ready for these kinds of parties, and it was always an extreme form of punishment (so to speak) on me. I had to scrub the house top to bottom, plan activities and shop to have a party at our house.

Besides silly games that we made up for entertainment, we also arranged for a family "talent show." The boys thought it was stupid, but had no choice except to participate in the planning. Chad, being rather competitive, wanted ours to be the best, and we spent the days after Christmas rehearsing an extreme version of "Cirque de Heller," a series of random "talents" we each had set to music and various acrobatic moves. The rehearsals, though well intended, became stressful and ugly. Tempers rose as six different people who all had different ideas tried to plan. In addition to preparing for the talent show, Chad put together a list of cleaning jobs that needed to get done in order to have the house in good showing condition. This part of him always reminded me of my mother in that appearances mattered so much; growing up, I can remember few times when people came over to our house, yet I remember enough to know that my mom always wanted everything presentable so that their first impression would be favorable in her mind.

As New Year's Eve got closer, I remember frantically trying to accomplish all the tasks on his list, including using a toothbrush to scrub every inch of baseboard in the house. On my hands and knees, I painstakingly got that job done; for some reason, just thinking about doing it still makes me angry (at myself) for following his orders that way. The afternoon of the party, before any guests had arrived, we got into a huge fight—over what, I cannot recall—and spent a very long time shouting at each other while the boys hid upstairs in their rooms. At party time, as the guests started to arrive, we all had smiles on our faces and successfully (I think) pretended that this party had brought us hours of pleasure in preparation.

The winter months of 2007 came and went. Our marriage continued to decline; arguing, profanity, distrust, belittling, and him viewing pornography were daily events. The religious growth had stopped, but his religious rhetoric continued. Sex became a threat for me to use on him, and an excuse for him to recite submission passages from the Bible to me.

It was not uncommon for him to mistreat me all evening long, but then approach me for sex at bedtime. If I turned down his advances, our family was usually guaranteed a couple of hours of him slamming doors and yelling, until he would simply get his computer, find a porn site and take care of his needs. This became the norm. Those nights, I usually got very little sleep, and the aftermath would last until the next night, when it was repeated. Two or three times a week, I'd muster up enough strength to have sex with him, all the while feeling less filled and more used, but it kept peace on those nights, so I did it.

During the first months that I was learning about his unfaithfulness, I had a few moments of rage. I recall smashing a bunch of plates one night after an argument at dinner; the boys sat at the table and watched me screaming at their dad while one plate after another was reduced to chips of stone. After those early months passed, I became so numb to sex and love that I never got angry anymore. I'm sure these things planted themselves in my heart, because through my healing process, I've had to sort through them to define my own dream of what love and sex would look like in a healthy relationship. But during the later parts of our marriage, I was simply flat-lined in that arena. I think Chad knew, and that frustrated him, but I didn't get much patience or compassion from him.

V - Summer 2007

By the summer of 2007, I was slipping into a depression. I had reached a point of needing to take naps during the day, and was finding very little joy in doing much of anything. My hope for a happy marriage had become hopelessness. I was consumed with thoughts of the affairs and my own feelings of inadequacy. I began getting counseling from a therapist in a neighboring community and slowly started to find my way out, at least temporarily. That summer, I renewed my teaching certification and started substitute teaching in the fall. My hope was to regain my own identity through doing something that I wanted to do instead of something my husband needed me to do.

It didn't work.

I filed for divorce in October. After arguing with myself for over two years, I finally shushed the voice telling me to keep trying, keeping that voice quiet long enough to take action. Telling the children, I simply tried to explain how hurt I was and that I wasn't sure I'd ever be able to look at their dad in the same way again.

I asked him to move out by the end of October. During the weekend that he was to move, I took the three younger boys camping for the weekend. Ben didn't want to come;

he was feeling sorry for Chad, and I didn't pressure him to join us. When I arrived home from that weekend, I went into the master bathroom and found literally every inch of wall space covered in yellow Post-it notes, each one with a red heart drawn on it. I can't even say that I thought for a moment that it was a sweet gesture; I think I was so shocked at the idea that he would do it, I didn't even know what to think. I did, however, know that it was going to take a long time to remove them.

Chad was still in and out of the house at that point, and he came into the bathroom while I was there, big smile on his face, and asked if I liked what he did.

I didn't even know how to respond. I believe I just looked at him, confused.

He stated that it took him several hours to complete, and it was the least he could do to show his love for me.

That was not the message I received. To me, it seemed like a show, a way for him to demonstrate to himself and everyone else how much he loved me.

In my mind, I had every intention of going through with the divorce, but the cries of my boys—mainly Ben—tugged at my heartstrings and caused me to rethink.

During the three months that divorce was imminent, Chad and I began seeing a psychologist for counseling. My motto was "Help us get divorced better," while Chad's motto was "Save our marriage."

The boys' pleas, the show of effort Chad was making, my pastor's words all had an impact on my resolve. In February of 2008, I called off the divorce and vowed to make the marriage work, somehow. I wish I could say that things got better, that we fell in love again, that he became a faithful servant leader for a husband.

I cannot.

We sustained the marriage by staying in exactly the same mindset we had been in for three years. I tolerated and rationalized his continuing pornography use, searches for women online, and mistreatment of me, and often the children (especially Gabe and Jordan). I decided that our marriage was never going to change, but since I had promised him for better or worse, I had to stay.

By the fall of 2010, Ben was off to college, I had been offered a full-time teaching position, and Chad decided to go back to college, majoring in psychology with the finish goal of becoming a family counselor.

I found myself longing for time away from Chad. I understand now what a huge red flag it is, but I didn't understand that at the time. I dreaded his return at night. Listening to his religious banter along with his newfound psychology vocabulary caused me to shudder whenever he started a rant (which happened more and more frequently).

Ben's baseball performance at college and Luke's activities during his senior year served as a distraction for us all, and gave a higher purpose to life than simply focusing on the bad state of our marriage.

As Luke prepared to go to college after high school graduation in 2011, I began to feel a panic within. Luke and I always had an understanding about each other; he instinctively always knew how I was feeling, and I him. We were affectionate and open in the way we talked and expressed love. He knew when I needed a hug and I knew when he needed me. Thinking about him being gone in a few months was causing apprehension about the loneliness that was coming for both of us, though I knew as a parent that I had to let him go and encourage him to find his place in the world. His graduation was difficult for me, more difficult than Ben's. I cannot be sure of this, but I honestly believe that my soul knew things were about to get worse at home, and I wasn't sure I had the strength to deal with it. Luke has an intuition about him that is different from anyone I've ever known. He instinctually knows when to come closer, when to give distance, and exactly what words will help calm any situation. I relied on that spirit of his; it helped keep me sane. And soon I would have to live without it.

That summer, Ben was asked to play in the Alaska Baseball League. He flew out on Memorial Day and three weeks later, Gabe, Jordan and I went out to join him and explore that state while touring in a small RV. Our trip to Alaska gave me renewed life for quite a while. Our time away from Chad was peaceful, and enjoying the beautiful scenery while deciding what to do each day without pressure or arguments was a delight. The boys and I bonded in a most precious way, and I'll never forget the feeling of realizing how small we were compared to the majesty of the mountains we were seeing. It was breathtaking. As I watched couples work together, love each other, and enjoy company, I found myself longingly thinking how nice it would be to have a vacation with a partner who loved me. Chad and I did a little texting during those two weeks. I remember him writing, complaining to me that he took Luke to a Twins game, and during the ride, Luke barely talked. He said he tried to start conversation, but Luke just didn't have much to say.

I got a mental picture immediately. Things had reached a point where I rarely started a conversation with Chad, and I believe at that time the kids felt much the same way. We all spent a great deal of energy simply trying to prevent their dad from getting mad. We were walking on eggshells, knowing that at any moment, the smallest hiccup could cause an avalanche. There was no place in our relationship for my feelings and perspectives. So, I knew any conversation I started would become an opportunity for Chad to talk and for me to listen. If I could adequately tell you how many hours of my life were spent listening to him talk at me, your jaw would drop.

His near constant use of Bible verses while he talked, combined with f-bombs and other foul language, usually made me confused over the contradictory messages. He was just so self-righteous; it galled me that he couldn't see his own hypocrisy. Every Sunday after two hours of church, he wanted to come home and talk about what we all learned. I do have vivid memories of one Sunday's sermon (the topic was unlearning); we got in the car after church and Chad said to me, "That sermon was about you, Bonnie."

Now, to his credit, I most definitely did need to unlearn some things. But who doesn't? The very idea that anyone would say something so brazen is ridiculous; the fact that he said it to me, and was completely serious, says more about him than me. It wasn't the only time something like this happened, and though I never told anyone about those kinds of things he said to me, I did wonder frequently if other husbands or wives said things like that to each other. My only hope for our sons was that they had the ability to understand that the way their dad treated me was not indicative of a respectful and loving relationship.

Luke left for college that August, and Ben came home from Alaska and left for college shortly after. The first six weeks without Luke around were brutal on me. I missed him terribly, yet I didn't want him to know how I felt. I held it in and tried to cling to the unconditional love that Gabe and Jordan were able to give to me.

In November, Chad expressed interest in taking a class to become marriage mentors through the church. These mentors "adopt" a couple (usually a young couple) and meet with them regularly to discuss marriage and the trials within. I'm not sure why he thought we'd be suited to serve in that capacity, but I speculate that he simply didn't understand the level at which our marriage was actually broken. I didn't think we'd be in any way capable, considering how I viewed our marriage, but the fact that Chad thought we would be good at it is very telling about his views on marriage, as well as what he considered success in that area.

I agreed to take the class; remember, I wanted to be able to say that I tried my best.

We had to read a book and then attend a weekend seminar; I read the book cover to cover, and planned on going to the seminar with Chad, but coming home from school on the Friday of the seminar, he began a rant about how dirty the house was and that he just spent half the day cleaning it. He told me he was trying to help me so that we could go to the meeting, but by that point, I was so frustrated, both at his yelling and at the idea that he thought I was, in addition to all the other adjectives he would call me, a bad homemaker. I just couldn't find the energy to put on a happy face and go through with this thing. I knew we'd be horrible at it anyway; I viewed our marriage as nothing short of a disaster.

Something got into me that day and I went with it; I think it was a small surge of independence. I grabbed my purse and drove the car to a nearby town. I bought a ticket to a movie and sat and watched a movie all by myself, leaving Chad at home with the kids. None of them knew where I was, and though I was worried about that, I simply couldn't be at home. It had gotten that bad. I remember being pissed beyond measure at the fact that I didn't want to be home. That's the one place in the world that people are supposed to feel peace. What I felt inside those four walls was anything but peaceful.

The next day, I woke up and drove, by myself, to Milwaukee to see Chad's brother and his wife. I told them everything that had happened, and they were good ears to spill it all to. They listened and reassured me that I was not crazy, remembering random times when Chad had reacted poorly to them or their kids. Neither of them could understand what was so hard about love.

I went back home late that night, assuring myself that the boys would be sleeping, and I crawled into bed. The next morning, Chad and the boys acted as though nothing had happened. We woke up, went to church, and had a usual Sunday. I have no idea why they didn't ask where I was, didn't show concern as to whether I was OK, didn't show any anger about me being gone. My leaving like that was out of character for me; it was one of only a few times during our marriage that I stood up for what I needed, and perhaps Chad was so taken back by my actions that he simply decided to not acknowledge them. Perhaps, in his mind, if he didn't acknowledge them, then the whole event never really happened. Validation was something he was never good at giving.

VI - January 2012

That winter, things began to get worse than ever. The atmosphere in the house was volatile and tense. I was almost at the point of looking strung out each workday, from lack of sleep due to Chad's rants in the middle of the night. The only way to avoid them was to have the sex I described earlier, leaving me empty and frustrated. He would frequently send me off to work after saying something mean to me. Though I was glad to get out of the house, I didn't perform well at my job because there was so much on my mind and heart. I was having trouble finding joy in much of anything, and the idea of living like that for the rest of my life was overwhelmingly depressing.

As he continued taking classes at the university, he began using what he had learned about psychology in conjunction with the Bible to try to "help" me. I was becoming repulsed by the words he spoke about God; the hypocrisy was so great that I simply didn't want to hear any more bullshit from him about how any of us should be living. I was beginning to question my own beliefs, which pissed me off even more.

I would never say that I was a devout Christian, a fundamentalist, or even a true follower; I did believe, however, and I always knew how to make decisions based on the teachings I had. I prayed, often. I listened to Christian music and always felt like Jesus loved me. But I had reached a point in all of this that I wasn't sure of anything anymore; things were getting out of control and I didn't know what to do. What I did know, though, was that Chad needed to stop. He needed to stop talking and start listening; he needed to ask me how I felt; he needed to gain a few specks of patience and empathy; he needed to walk like the man he was so good at talking himself into being. I had been praying for those qualities in him for years, as well as my own ability to love him the way God did, but nothing ever happened. I think that was part of my disconnect from God as well. I had so many people tell me to remain faithful, that God wants goodness in my life, and that when the time is right, He would make all things work together for my good, but I reached the point of giving up. I felt confused about

Chad's rhetoric, his preaching of words without actions…it all caused me to question everything at my very core.

One Sunday in April of that year, Chad was napping on the couch. His phone was in our bedroom, and I heard a series of text messages come in.

Out of curiosity, I looked at his phone, to discover a woman from one of his classes trying to make arrangements with him to have lunch and go see a movie together. I didn't say anything to Chad that day, but woke up the next morning just sick at the idea that he was still carrying on with other women despite all the counseling, despite the hurt his infidelity had already caused the family. I called the pastor that morning and asked him to meet with us, and told Chad he needed to come with.

Upon sitting down in Russ's office, I didn't talk too much at first. Russ simply asked him, "Do you realize that your wife is so distraught that she can't work today?"

Chad stared blankly at him. Russ repeated the question, as if to remind him that this was a big deal. He said, "Chad—are you on the prowl?"

Chad replied, "No, Russ. But obviously you two know something so why don't you just tell me what it is so that I can go back to work?"

Russ then nodded at me to speak. I explained the texts, the history searches on the computer, and my concern over him looking at escort and prostitute sites.

Chad got mad. He claimed he was just looking, that nothing happened, and that I should worry more about our marriage instead of spending my time spying on him. He said that I was, again, making a mountain out of a molehill.

Russ replied, "Chad, I believe you are trying to make a molehill out of a mountain."

At that, Chad stood up and left. We watched him drive off from the office window, as I sat in disbelief that my feelings mattered so little and that he didn't understand that this was a very big deal.

At that point, Russ didn't really know what to tell me. He simply said that he was sorry, and that I should be praying for guidance. He made no excuses about Chad; he knew the whole story very well and showed a great deal of compassion for the pain I had already endured, as well as what this must do to me psychologically.

I went home and started supper.

Months went by where I barely functioned. Work, supper, sex, sleep (a little), repeat. I was hopeless and frustrated about my marriage because nothing had changed, and my husband knew it. I didn't like him anymore, and I hated myself for not being able to articulate my needs and feelings. I felt trapped but somehow kept believing that there must have been something I could do—we could do—to make this marriage better. I continued having sex with him two or three nights a week, but I was less present during each time. This was frustrating to Chad, as he told me he wanted to have a connection with me, but I was so beaten down as a woman that I simply allowed him to do what was necessary, all the while understanding that the sex was something I had to endure if I wanted to get any sleep.

In late July, I took the younger boys on a two-day camping trip to spend some quality time with them before the new school year started.

VII - August 2012

Gabe, Jordan and I returned from our short camping trip on Friday. As we unpacked, I noticed a piece of paper in the garage that had the name of a motel, an address, and a telephone number on it. I went to the computer and did a little research. I can't say that I knew for sure, but based on the fact that I did know he had been looking online for sexual partners, I had an idea that this was proof that he actually went through with it. I was so sick at the idea that I couldn't talk about it. I knew there would be a time for that, but I had to process and get the courage up to face him. I knew that when I asked him about it, he would either deny and tell me I was crazy, or he would find a way to blame me. I needed to be ready for both responses.

Three days later, early Monday morning, I woke up and poured my coffee. All four boys were home and still sleeping. I went to the screened-in porch, where Chad was, and I sat down. The first words out of my mouth that morning were, "What is the Edgewood Motel?"

He repeated, "The Edgewood Motel?"

"Yes," I said.

"Oh. I went there for a massage," he replied.

"A massage? At a motel?" I asked, looking at him with a confused sort of blank stare.

"Well, it was a massage with a happy ending," he stated.

"A happy ending? Chad—you hired a prostitute?" I asked, in response to his matter-of-fact statement.

He replied, "An escort, not a prostitute. And you could have prevented it if you and Russ hadn't gotten me so riled up back in April." (In reference to the meeting in which our pastor and I confronted him about his searches for prostitutes and ongoing dialogue with other women).

There it was. The blame.

At that moment, I swear, something happened inside me. It was like God himself came down and whispered, "It's time for you to go, Bonnie. There's nothing more you can do. Go." I was done. Things were never going to change, and I knew I had to leave him.

I simply picked up my coffee cup, walked a few steps, turned around and said, "You call yourself a man."

I went to my bedroom, heart beating a million miles an hour, and called Pastor Russ. He was on vacation for the week, so he told me to call the assistant pastor, which I did. I also called Bill, the psychologist we had seen a few years before. I told them both what had happened, and explained that I needed to meet with them as soon as possible. I had specific questions for both of those people, but neither could see me for a couple of days.

I spent the next several hours wandering aimlessly around the house, weeping, understanding that my life was about to change. Chad followed me from room to room, telling me I'd get through it, that divorce couldn't be an option, and that he would change. He also reminded me that God hates divorce, and that I would rot in hell if I divorced him. He was relentless. At one point, after asking him to leave me alone, he followed me out to the garage, where I turned around, called him a string of profanities and then stated, "Waste of human sperm, Chad? I am a waste of human sperm? NO! You are!" and with that, I smacked him with both hands on his cheeks probably ten times. I then spit on him, started bawling, and walked away.

As I walked away, he said, "I deserved that."

Somewhere in this nightmare, Chad called the boys outside for a meeting.

Gabe told me later that day that during the meeting, Chad explained what he had done and told the kids that I was really upset, but they needed to understand that since I wasn't a virgin when we got married, I was partly to blame. At this, Gabe got up, said, "Dad, if you say another word I'm going to punch you in the nose," and walked away. The other boys heard him out, and we never spoke of their conversation with him.

The next day, I went to get my questions answered.

For the pastor: "Will I go to hell if I divorce him?"

For Bill: "Is there hope that he will ever change?"

Russ came home from his vacation and met me at a local coffee shop. He knew that Chad did a lot of Bible thumping and finger pointing at me, and that his fundamentalist views were extreme. A large part of cancelling the divorce in 2007 came down to the fact that in the Bible, God says, "I hate divorce." Explaining everything that had happened and telling Russ my worries about going to hell if I divorced Chad, he said to me, "Bonnie. God hates divorce, yes. But do you know what God hates more? He hates the way that Chad treats you. He hates the way he makes you feel. He hates how he uses the Bible as a weapon to manipulate you and justify him. He hates that Chad has never been faithful to you. He hates that this was never a marriage to begin with. He hates those things, and He understands that sometimes, divorce is better than staying married."

Bill, the psychologist, wanted to see us both. Chad agreed, and we drove the hour to meet him at his office. We sat down, and within thirty seconds Bill said, "Tell me what you did, Chad."

At that, Chad stated that he hired an escort to give him a massage with a happy ending.

Bill reworded what he said: "So Chad, you hired a prostitute for sex?"

Chad replied, "No, I hired an escort for a massage with a happy ending."

Bill said, "So in other words, you hired a prostitute for sex."

Chad adamantly stated that she was an escort, while Bill tried to drive home the fact that when you pay for sex, it's considered prostitution.

This banter went on for probably five minutes until Bill asked how he managed to do that, since prostitution in Wisconsin is illegal.

Chad explained that he searched online, found offers, chose one he liked and made an appointment.

Bill then stated, "OK, let me get this straight. You looked online, found a willing woman, called her number, set up an appointment, agreed on a place, took out money, found directions to the motel, showered, got dressed, drove there, did it, and came back home?"

Chad said, "Yes."

Bill asked, "At what point did you stop and consider the possible effects this would have on your wife and children?"

Chad said, "I didn't think about that. I wanted to get my dick wet."

I told Chad the next morning that I would be moving out of the house as soon as I could, and I would be taking the boys. I told him that I planned to file for divorce. My marriage was doomed from the beginning and I never saw it coming. Legal documents show that we were married from July 1990 until May 2013. I left my husband in August of 2012; upon finding out about the paid services, I knew I had no other choice. Whoever that woman was, she would be the last other woman.

Seven years of separations, threats of divorce, newfound religion and marriage counseling clearly didn't cure his need to stray, and this was the proverbial straw on that camel's back.

I broke.

I knew that if I didn't get out, the stress of being married to him was going to kill me. And so, with a little over two hundred dollars in my checking account, two kids and a dog, I moved out.

The demise of our marriage had come to fruition.

Chapter 2

Giant Red Letters

I – August 2012

It is not my place to discuss the relationship any of my boys have with their dad. I will only say that I believe they were massively confused, mostly because they loved me so much. I think they couldn't wrap their brains around the way their dad treated me. It didn't make sense to them why he didn't love me. They were angry and they were tired of seeing me cry. When I mentioned to Gabe and Jordan that I was leaving their dad, both of them reacted with words something along the lines of "Well, it's about time."

That was affirming. Yet, as a schoolteacher, I have been around children long enough to know that no child, no matter how bad his parents' marriage is, wants to see them get a divorce. That understanding was one of the main reasons I did not leave him earlier. I hated the idea that my kids were going to come from what society calls a "broken home," but the truth was this: their home was broken already. I was just going to make it formal. During discussions that I had with each of my children, I vowed to myself that I could not let my love for them be a weakness to change my mind. Ben's pleas to keep our family together caused me to cancel the divorce in 2008, and the marriage only got worse after that. I couldn't risk any more wasted time trying to repair a marriage that never existed in the first place. I knew that if I stayed, nothing would ever change. I would complete my life sentence of feeling like I was never enough for the man I called my husband.

The last couple of weeks that I lived in the house while planning my departure were difficult at best for all of us. Chad continued working; I continued taking care of the house and getting ready for the new school year, the boys tiptoed around us. We were all stage actors in a drama whose curtains had closed long ago. The environment there was nothing short of awful. He tried to convince the children that I was making a huge mistake and that he would change his behavior; I avoided conversation until a verbal explosion could be restrained no more. I remember many dinners in which the children and I sat in silence while we listened to him scare us into thinking we were financially doomed, their college education would not be funded, and I would be left to die alone. I rebutted once he was out of the room with telling them that I'd work three jobs if I had to. And, I would rather die alone than to be with someone who didn't love me. I would stand at the sink washing dishes while tears streamed down both cheeks, questioning my ability to live without him but resolving that I was going to try, even if it killed me. We both counted down the days, him trying to get us to stay, and me ready to run for the hills.

I went to the doctor at the urging of my sister Karen, who is a nurse. I had made an appointment for a pap smear, knowing that I would have to tell the doctor what was going on, but not wanting to say it over the phone to the receptionist.

Upon sitting down in the examination room, the doctor walked in. I immediately started to sob. He asked what was going on, and in between breaths, I managed to simply say, "My husband was with a prostitute and I need you to check me for STDs. I have filed for divorce."

The doctor was completely professional and didn't mention any of this to the nurse as they did the exam. He simply said, "Bonnie's having a rough day. Let's do this quickly." I recall lying on the examination table feeling utterly humiliated. Never in my life did I imagine I'd need to get an exam of this kind.

It felt like being cheated on with a prostitute was the lowest of lows. Don't mistake me—infidelity hurts no matter who it is done with. The idea that he was willing to pay someone to take my place in bed was just a huge punch in the gut. I had longed to be loved. For years, I knew that if only he could love me, I would have been putty in his hands. I realized that day at the doctor that he'd rather pay money to have someone take my place in bed than invest in caring for my heart; I wasn't worth the investment.

I later discovered that while I was at the doctor getting checked for an infection, Chad was at home calling our mutual fund managers. Chad emptied our retirement and college savings accounts of $43,000 (for which he would later be charged with contempt). I didn't find out about this until my lawyer, Wally, was going through our finances. Chad never mentioned this to me and successfully managed to hide the money. Some went to Luke for college expenses, but much of it remains unaccounted for. I was most upset about the fact that he did it while I was getting checked for STDs that *he* could have given me. Again, his priority and investment in our marriage was reduced to money. It reminded me exactly where I stood with him.

In a way, Chad's dalliance with prostitution served as a fuel for me. Through the proceedings, the betrayal propelled me to stay firm in the decision I had made. I had been told by a close family member to "get ready because this is going to be the hardest thing you'll ever do. You're about to divorce the biggest bully any of us has ever known."

Sadly, that was not the hardest thing I would ever endure, but I can tell you it was exhausting in every possible way.

To be honest, I'll admit that there were many times during our divorce that I wished he would just man up and take ownership of what he'd done, because I would have gone back to him. I do believe that if he'd been able to muster up some empathy and show some concern for me and for his children, I would have reconsidered.

I viewed divorce as a major failure and it was not how my picture of life was supposed to be; there were times that I projected what it would be like for him to humbly come to me and admit his mistake and validate the pain it had caused me. That fictional scenario always ended with a big hug and the two of us walking off together into the sunset. The fairy tale had a once upon a time, a bunch of ugly shit in the middle of the story, and a happily ever after. It seemed delusional yet feasible somewhere in my mind.

But Prince Charming never did appear. Instead, I began to see a side of Chad I knew was there but had never completely experienced. His attempts at getting me to reconsider only made me more determined… and more afraid of what would happen if I reconsidered. I was changing into a woman who wanted to take back her life.

The boys and I moved out at the end of August 2012, and rented the home of a friend in town, just down the street from the high school. The first night we were there, I made spaghetti without meat and we ate from paper plates while sitting on the family room floor. The contrast from where we had just been, a beautiful house with chairs… I felt like a horrible mother, wondering how I was ever going to support the boys on my salary and whether I had made the right decision. I began to cry, and I apologized to Gabe and Jordan about both our new living conditions and the meal.

Gabe looked at me and said, "Mom, this is the best meal I've ever eaten." Jordan nodded. I could find no words to respond to the beauty of what they had just given me.

A week later was our first court hearing. The purpose of it was to arrange for temporary placement of the kids during the mandatory wait time until the divorce could be final. It would mark the first of many court hearings in which the outcome favored the children and my wishes.

Primary placement, as requested by the children, was given to me. In hiring Wally as my lawyer, I told him I only needed him to represent my children; that day in court he proved that he was doing just that, and my kids were given some consistency and shown that they would be listened to. I think the three of us felt a little validated on that day.

A week later, Wally called to let me know that Chad had hired a new lawyer and asked for a de novo hearing. That means that he disagreed with the outcome of court and wanted a new hearing with a different judge. Wally told me not to worry, that we'd do exactly what we did the first time, and that the judge would likely side the same way. He did want me to know that Chad was seeking 50/50 placement and a reduction in the amount of child support he was paying.

The hearing was scheduled for October.

II – October 2012

I thought that once I moved out, things would get easier. I was wrong.

Two people could not have done a worse job of divorcing.

He was pissed; I was determined. He wanted control; I wanted freedom.

For months, we sent long and arduous text messages back and forth, and he wrote to the children. He filled their ears with negativity and shit talk about me, and I am ashamed to say that I reacted with shit talk of my own each time I learned what he was saying. He began to tell the children that I was "divorcing the family." He began referring to me as "Bonnie" instead of "Mom" when he spoke to them. He reminded them of our wedding vows and that I promised to stay with him for better or for worse. I got defensive. I would remind the children what he did.

I spent a great deal of time trying to tell my children what a healthy marriage should look like. Interrupting a perfectly normal dinner conversation, I made random statements to my boys like, "You do know that the way your dad treated me is not how a man should treat a woman, right?" or "Promise me now that you will NEVER treat a woman the way your dad treated me!" I know; I probably seemed a little unhinged to them. I had begun to worry that his messages to the kids were going to become their truth, especially since they were so one-way—like a subliminal message at movie theaters where iridescent words come on the screen saying, "You want popcorn." The only way I knew how to repel those messages from their minds was to fill them with my idea of the truth.

I look back now and feel awful about both our behavior.

A few months after I had left, I read something regarding the process of divorce that said, "You have to love your children more than you hate your spouse."

Around that time, Gabe came home from a weekend and told me about a conversation he had with his dad. Gabe said, "Dad, don't you think this is the most expensive prostitute that was ever hired?" His dad asked what he meant.

Gabe replied, "Well, your wife has left you. Your kids only come to your house every other week. You have to pay child support and you have to buy your own food. You're spending a lot of money on lawyers. Your wife pays rent to live somewhere else while you stay in this huge house by yourself. I feel like that's a huge price to pay."

I sat there in awe and realized at that moment that there was nothing else I needed to say to my kids. They knew. They understood. And I wanted to be the mom that loved her kids more than she hated her spouse; I knew I already did, but I vowed that I would prove it to them.

From that time forward, I implemented a "no contact" rule with Chad. I tried to respond only to communication that was in regard to the children. I wasn't perfect at it, but I found power in having the ability to disregard messages that were meant to rile me up, and over time, those messages simply stopped coming. I guess there's some wisdom in the advice people give to children when they tell them that a bully will give up when they learn they can't upset you. As for finding power in disregarding? It actually helped me with my self-confidence; I began to understand that I was not just something to be tossed around like a balloon in a game of "keep it off the ground," but instead, I could choose what I wanted to get upset about. He didn't have that power over me anymore; I had taken it away.

One side note here: I don't believe for a moment that Chad tried to end our marriage. I honestly don't think it ever crossed his mind that I would leave. I had turned my cheek to his behavior and given him so many second chances that I was in essence giving him permission to do whatever he wanted. So his response of shock and anger to my leaving was, looking back, expected.

Three days before that de novo hearing, I got a phone call at six o'clock in the morning. There was a sheriff's deputy on the line, telling me that Chad had spent several hours in his office the night before, and was accusing me of assault, from the day that I had smacked him in the face after he followed me around the house telling me I couldn't divorce him.

I remember thinking to myself, "How was I married to this man for twenty-two years? I don't even know who he is."

We agreed to meet in my school parking lot to discuss the matter. Meanwhile, Gabe and Jordan overheard the whole conversation and were both upset and worried that I might wind up in jail that day. I told them I'd be making them dinner that night and gave them both a kiss and a hug, telling them I had faith that the truth would prevail.

I called Wally and he told me to tell the deputy exactly what had happened; he reminded me that I had nothing to hide. Arriving at school, I pulled in next to the deputy, he got out of his squad car, and we introduced ourselves. I told him exactly what had happened that day, from beginning to end, including the smack, the spit, and the words I had said. His response was jaw dropping.

He simply said, "This is not assault. What happened was this…you reached your capacity for torment and you snapped. Chad confessed to the prostitute last night, adding that 'It's just what soldiers do.' I'm going to call Chad and tell him no charges will be filed. Then I'm going to call Wally and tell him that I'd be happy to testify in court to tell the judge exactly what Chad said and how you reacted. Don't worry, Bonnie. It's all going to be OK."

Hearing the last part—"It's all going to be OK"—loosened the knot I'd had in my stomach from the last two hours. I thought, "Hell—if a law enforcement officer can see what's really going on here then I can relax a little." I knew the truth and so did Chad. He was going to do anything in his power to regain control, and my only job was to not worry and to tell the truth. Everything else would work out as it should.

I walked into school a half hour late and the school secretary said to me, "Go home, Bonnie. We called a substitute for you…you can't be expected to function properly after having to start your day like that."

Until that point, I had tried to keep my personal life separate from my job. Two teacher friends at school knew the situation, and were a constant source of support and good ears to lean on, but my students had no idea what was going on (and I never did tell them). My boss and other fellow staff members only knew that I was getting a divorce. But that day, I realized that they knew more than I had ever told them. They had my back, and I began to feel the support they wanted to give to me and to my children.

At the de novo hearing, we had a real judge (not a commissioner like the first hearing). Chad had since fired his first lawyer and gotten a new one. The judge heard both sides, almost verbatim from the first hearing, and asked some questions. He wanted to know why Chad told the kids about the affairs and the prostitute, he wanted to know who did the majority of the parental tasks when we were living together, and he wanted to know how the kids felt. By this time, a GAL (guardian ad litem) and a custody evaluator had been assigned by the courts, and both had interviewed the kids.

The outcome of that hearing was exactly the same as the first.

I recall thinking to myself after it was over, "The courts can see. This really is going to be OK."

When I came home from court that day, Gabe and Jordan wanted to know the outcome. When I told them that everything would stay the same for now, Gabe said, "Mom, I want to go and hug Wally."

I thought about that statement for a few days until I mentioned it to Wally at our next meeting. I said, "Wally—Gabe told me he wants to hug you. I think he feels like you're really investing in his wellbeing."

Wally replied, "No. For the first time in his life, he sees a man standing up for you. He wants to hug me because he likes the way that feels."

I think Wally was right.

During the next few months, we began to learn a new normal. Every Tuesday we'd go to the local Chinese restaurant and order food to take home. I loved when the boys would come downstairs to breakfast and mention that they couldn't wait for dinner on those nights.

Both boys had become interested in a card game called "Magic the Gathering." Some nights, they'd sit at the kitchen table and play while I watched in confusion. A few times, they tried (unsuccessfully) to teach me how to play. I never did grasp the rules of the game—all those wizards and angels were too much for me to keep track of—but I loved the way we all tried to be a little family, and I think it meant a lot to them, too.

Jordan, 15 years old at the time, saw a need to hang some speakers in the family room and rode his bike to Walmart one day to buy screws, then came home and hung them up. I remember thinking how proud I was that he did that all by himself, with his own money and by his own ambition.

Gabe was getting ready for a dance one night and we didn't have an iron, so he heated up a pan and tried to iron with it. He scorched the shirt, but I recall feeling immense joy at the way he tried to make do with what we had.

A little while after that, he was invited to go on a two-day field trip to Milwaukee and needed dress clothes to wear. When he asked me to take him shopping, I told him I only had $20 to spare, and he suggested we go to Goodwill. We did, and as I helped him spend $19 on three new sets of clothes, I remember thanking him for his incredible attitude regarding the whole situation.

From the courts' perspective, the goal of divorce is that all family members should be able to maintain their way of life. That was not the case in our situation. Rent and energy bills alone took more than one entire paycheck each month. Between a credit card payment, food, gas, school lunches and insurance payments, I was living paycheck to paycheck even with child support coming in at that time.

I had to say no to many requests that the boys had, but they clearly didn't care. They wanted peace—not name brand clothes—and there were glimpses of hope that they were beginning to find it.

I used the benefit of a reduced fee for the gym through the wellness program in our school district to go work out with Gabe and Jordan several times a week, and I used some money my dad had given me (with strict instructions to buy something *I* wanted) to take pottery classes. All four boys seemed to find joy in cheering me on in my new endeavors, while I tried to create a sense of home for them.

Indeed, it seemed as though things were getting better a little at a time.

III – December 2012

People who knew Chad for a long time understood that he had a temper. Because of employee relations and his reputation in the community for being somewhat of a hothead, once word got out that I had moved out of the house, there was some community concern. Within a week of us moving, I began noticing police cars slowly driving past the house we were living in, several times a day. A few times at night, I woke up to see a police car shining a spotlight on our house while driving slowly. I inquired about this and was told that all of the officers were instructed to keep an eye on my property.

In December of that year, the Connecticut school shooting happened. My principal saw me in the hallway after school that day and mentioned it to me. The next week, sheriff's deputies began showing up at my school and doing walk-throughs a few times each day. I asked my principal what was going on, and he explained that since the shooting, administration and the sheriff's department had discussed my separation from Chad, and since they'd had experience with him before, were a little worried and decided that extra protection might be a prudent idea. They came up with a plan to get me to safety if he should ever enter the school building, and to this day, they still walk the halls at least once each day.

The protection I was receiving, as well as the fact that I was being cared for in that way, caused me to feel safe yet also highly on guard, obsessive about where the keys to the house were, whether the doors were locked, and so forth. I've eased up quite a bit in that area, but I am still careful. My boys did not know about any of this. I didn't want them to know I was scared of their dad and I certainly didn't want them to be.

IV - May 9, 2013

We arrived a few minutes before the hearing. The judge swore us in. He asked me some basic questions and I answered; he did the same for Chad.

Once the formalities were over, the gavel echoed off the polished surfaces of the courtroom, and the divorce was granted. It took ten minutes in court to dissolve 22 years of marriage, and while that may seem to diminish the institution of our marriage, to me it seemed quite fitting. In the eyes of God, our marriage never existed in the first place; ten minutes was actually generous.

I did expect, however, to have emotions after the finalization. I wasn't sure what I'd feel—freedom, sadness, regret—but I thought I would feel something.

I did not.

I remember sitting there and feeling absolutely nothing. I signed the papers and I left. I stopped at the grocery store on my way home. Nothing felt different. I was surprised by that. On my way to the grocery store, I recall thinking that perhaps my inability to feel was, in fact, a sign that the whole divorce was just as simple as turning the last page in a book that I really hadn't enjoyed reading.

I do, however, remember thinking that day about the feelings my kids might be having. I didn't ask them, simply because I didn't want to introduce more drama into their lives. I do know that Chad sent them each a text message, stating that after 22 years of hard work, all can be lost in a moment. Gabe told me about it, and I guess at that moment I understood that what Chad lived and what I lived were two very different versions of the same marriage.

One of the biggest responsibilities of being a parent to boys is to teach them how to be a good husband. I had always known this, yet hardly a day went by that I didn't wonder what I was actually teaching them. I mean, I knew I was showing them how to keep a promise, but I worried that I also might be teaching them that a woman will put up with pretty much anything. That scared me and continues to be my greatest worry in all that they witnessed. So many times during or after an argument or an inappropriate comment, I'd pull the boys aside and tell them it wasn't OK for their dad to say or do what he did, asking them if they understood, and trying to help them see that it hurt me. But I never had the balls to just say to Chad's face, "Stop!"

I let my fear control me, and that is my biggest regret.

I recently heard a man say, "I got a divorce from a marriage I was never a part of."

Touché. I was never part of the marriage. To this day, I am aware that Chad says things to the children and others in regard to marriage being a lifelong commitment. In his eyes, I gave up.

In my eyes, I was never his wife to begin with—all those women he invited into our marriage took my place. I have a picture in my head of our marriage on a piece of paper.

Over it, in giant red letters, is a VOID stamp.

Chapter 3

A Hurricane's Eye

I - June 2013

In the months following the divorce, things settled down quite a bit and it seemed as though my children's lives were coming together in many ways.

Ben graduated college and was drafted in the twenty-second round of the major league baseball draft. The fruition of that dream wasn't a road paved in gold; his good decision-making skills and raw determination are what got him noticed. His story began at age one, when my parents took us to a supper club and he grabbed a dinner roll from the table and threw it across the room with such velocity that it hit a man sitting twenty feet or so away from us in the forehead. As a young boy, he played t-ball on a recreational team at a local park once a week. His legacy from that year was picking dandelions in right field and making Dixie Jo, a girl from his team, his first sweetheart. In middle school, he became more enthused about organized sports and began playing on a traveling baseball team, finding his way in the ranks by being patient when he asked if he could pitch but was denied, and instead spent most of his time on the bench. When he was finally allowed on the mound, Coach was happily surprised with what he saw and Ben began to pitch more frequently. By high school, he had quit any other sports he was in and focused only on baseball, even during the off-season, stating that his goal was to play college ball. I once heard him say, "Go big or go home." I realize he didn't coin that phrase, but I thought to myself how appropriately it summed up his mode of operation in life.

In high school, Ben was considered both a nerd and a dreamer—the nerd part likely came from a day when that six-foot boy left class in a hurry to be the first one in line for lunch. As he briskly walked the halls toward the cafeteria, he blew a whistle to get everyone out of his way. He wanted to be sure to get the Stromboli that day. It might have come from a failed attempt to teepee a friend's house when he left several pieces of paper showing the name and address of one of his cohorts, causing a Milwaukee news channel to come do a story on the prank gone terribly wrong. It might have been the way he never cussed and never drank, and found pleasure in playing board games or eating Chinese food on Friday nights instead of going to parties. The dreamer part came from the idea that he wanted to play baseball. Period. While he had a good arm, the idea that he wanted a future in sports gave others a reason to respond with "Pfft…"

But with the constant support and daily practicing with his brother, Luke, and a close friend of his, Rory, Ben honed his abilities for college and performed well enough while there that he was prepped to be drafted in the spring of his junior year.

When he wasn't picked up, Ben was devastated, wondering if his dream of playing professional baseball was out of touch and a waste of time and energy. It didn't take much reflection for Ben to decide that he would go back to school for his senior year and give the draft one more chance that following spring.

Meanwhile, he had fallen deeply in love with Martha, a beautiful woman he met at college, and became engaged to her during his senior year (which, as you recall, was also the year I left his dad). Meeting her for the first time, I thought to myself, "She's the one. He's going to marry that girl."

When he asked Martha's dad for his approval to take his daughter's hand, Ben found himself assuring the man that he would be faithful and loyal to her and to their marriage. I believe it was during those talks and because of his desire to make her his wife that Ben began to understand how broken my marriage was, and the truth that no one should be made to feel incidental in any partnership.

Planning for their wedding, Martha moved out to Phoenix for the summer to begin establishing a home for them while Ben stayed in the Midwest until the draft was over, knowing that the results would determine his next course in life.

Ben's role in the family was actually that of peacemaker. He wanted everyone to get along, all the time. He avoided conflict at the expense of his own ego, because he wanted calm, he wanted peace, and he wanted love; he was experiencing all of those things during those months.

My second-born, Luke, grew up as Ben's best friend and has the same mindset for justice, integrity, passion and love. During Luke's freshman year of college (one year before I left his dad), Luke became homesick and started questioning the integrity of the boys on his college baseball team. Every player had to sign a covenant agreement, stating he wouldn't participate in certain activities. Luke obeyed with no problem, but he watched as some players blatantly broke the rules and the coach turned a blind eye. He decided that he didn't want to be part of that and transferred to a small college in Michigan for the remainder of his education. He quickly felt a sense of belonging and developed a deep respect for the assistant coach of his team, who would be the most powerful adult role model Luke would ever know. During the summer following the finalization of the divorce, he played for a traveling baseball team but came home whenever he could, spending time with Gabe and Jordan and falling deeply in love with Anne, a woman he met at his new school. I recall meeting her and thinking the same thing as I did with Martha; I could see in his eyes how much he loved her, and I knew that one day, he would ask for her hand in marriage.

I recall a visit that summer on a day when Gabe and Jordan were scheduled to be with their dad. Luke would follow them from house to house in order to maximize the time he got with them, pouring his love and good example into them. This day, they were running a little late and

Chad texted them all, telling them to hurry up because they were wasting time. This got Gabe and Jordan a little tense. Luke calmly asked his dad to settle down and brought the boys there shortly after. I remember looking at him that day and being so proud of how he could feel what Gabe and Jordan were feeling and have the courage to stand up for them. Here's the thing...Luke had always been quiet. So quiet, in fact, that two weeks after he started kindergarten, his teacher called to let me know he hadn't spoken a single word during school. I chuckled and assured her that when he had something to say, he'd say it. Luke wasn't the kind of kid that wanted to fill the air with fluff. So when he spoke, people listened.

Jordan opened his own lawn care business that summer and started hanging out with a group of kids who didn't have the best decision-making skills. He got himself into some trouble, but as I watched him work his way out of it I believed he was learning some valuable life lessons, with the help of Gabe's disappointment and insightful advice for how to be a good person.

Gabe worked for a local farmer and was an umpire for the local recreation department's baseball and softball leagues. I took the boys camping a couple of times and as the summer wound down, we all got ready for a new school year.

II - September 2013

The boys and I settled into some routines while we all tried to work for our future. They loved having me come home from school and tell them stories of what my students did that day; I loved hearing their stories of shenanigans that went on at the high school.

In October of that year, Ben and Martha got married and he joined her in Phoenix. For Christmas that year, Luke, Anne, Gabe, Jordan and I drove out there to be with them. We made wonderful memories and to this day we like to tell stories of that happy, life-affirming adventure. In the months following, Luke became a captain of his baseball team at college and continued pursuing Anne, while we all seemed to be finding our way in life. I was very proud of the men my boys were becoming, even though they had a way of reminding me that they were still little boys at heart.

In January of 2014, Gabe figured out a way to e-mail every student in his grade. He wrote some kind of a joke with instructions to "reply all" with the word "yes." Students followed his instructions, causing the server to clog and the computer system to shut down for a time that day at the high school. When the assistant principal called me to let me know that Gabe would be serving a suspension, he confidentially told me that in his years he'd seen many pranks, but this one was by far the most brilliant.

Gabe found his place on the tennis team that year and continued questioning his teachers, until one of them requested that the school board pay for him to take a college-level computer class at the local university for the following fall—his senior year—because (I paraphrase) he knew more than she was able to teach him. He got a part-time job at Taco Bell and got his first girlfriend; it was sweet to watch the two of them in their innocent phase of first love.

He flourished in the fine arts, in athletics, not so much. But somehow he found his niche and a role within the team, and he felt like he belonged. One day, early on in tennis season his first year, he wore a *Captain America* t-shirt to practice. It was blue and had a bull's eye logo right in the center on the front with a big star inside. When his teammates saw him wearing that, they decided he'd be perfect target practice and they began aiming their tennis balls right at his chest. He pretended for a little while to be annoyed by it, but he began wearing that shirt many times each week and every time he did, he was the target. While he wasn't one of the star players on the team, he was important and he knew it. His silly demeanor was appreciated by every player on that team. One day, he left to go to the bathroom inside the school. When he came out, all of the players were lined up against the backstop and the coach was facing them, yelling at them like coaches sometimes do. Gabe saw this and walked in from the back gate, went to the net behind the coach, and pulled down his pants, scurrying back and forth along the net, mooning the whole team. Coach began to raise his voice even more when his players were giggling, and Gabe was never caught. It was so daring, so completely unexpected, that for Gabe's teammates, it will be one of those moments in life they'll never forget.

That spring (still his junior year), he came home from school one day really upset about something that had happened during one of his classes. Waiting for the other students to answer a question posed by the teacher regarding what the value of absolute zero was, he spoke up and correctly stated that it had no value because it was an imaginary number. To that, the teacher replied, "Yes. It's imaginary, just like all of your friends."

Gabe told me that afternoon that he slumped down in his chair and tried to refrain from crying because he felt so humiliated, as the class erupted in laughter at the teacher's comment. My heart was broken for him that day.

Later that night, I e-mailed the teacher and told him how Gabe felt, and with sincere humility, that teacher apologized to Gabe the following day. I witnessed a grown man show my child what it means to really "man up" and for that, I am thankful. I should also note that Gabe and that teacher went on to develop a healthy, mutually respectful relationship from that point on.

One night shortly after that, Gabe came home from a friend's house and I was already in bed. I heard him come in and climb the stairs. He got his pajamas on and briskly but quietly crawled into my bed, wrapped his arm around me and spooned me.

He said, "Mom, I have to tell you something. I got high tonight."

I can't say I wasn't disappointed, shocked, pissed or a combination of all three of those feelings, but having been a teenager once myself, I decided I wasn't going to get mad.

I turned over, turned on the light and said, "Hmm. Well, OK then. This is your free pass. Weed is illegal and we are not lawbreakers, so this won't happen again, all right?"

I then asked him how it felt and where he did it and who gave it to him. He told me everything and when he was done, he went into his own room and went to bed.

I never suspected that he was smoking again until about three months later, when I came home early from a school meeting, walked in the house, and smelled it.

I called him downstairs and asked him what the smell was. He looked at me and said he didn't smell anything.

I believe my next words were something along the lines of "How stupid do you think I am," and then I marched up to his room and threatened to tear apart everything inside until I found what I was looking for. He knew I was serious, so he pulled out a bag from under his bed and handed it to me. Inside, I found a pipe and a Ziploc baggie full of weed. First, I asked him where he got it. After some hesitation, he told me the kid's name.

Then I took that baggie, emptied it into the sink and turned on the garbage disposal and watched it all go away. He watched too. I hit the pipe with a meat mallet and threw the shards of glass in the garbage can.

Then I sent a message to the boy who sold him the pot and told him that if he ever supplied my son with drugs again, I would report him to the police.

When I was finished, he looked at me with tears in his eyes and said, "You're a bitch."

He had never, NEVER called me a name before. Ever. I was hurt, yes, but I knew he was saying things simply because he was mad, so I didn't exacerbate the situation by doing or saying anything. I just stood there looking at him with disappointment in my eyes. He never did apologize, but his friends told me later that he told them all about it and said he felt awful for calling me that name.

One night (still at the age of 17) after he was out on a date, Gabe came home, put on his pajamas and again crawled into the bed with me. He put his arm around me and spooned me. I turned over and looked at him.

He said, "Mom, I have to tell you something. I kissed a girl tonight."

I smiled and thought to myself how lucky I was to be the one person he wants to share this with, and then asked him how it felt.

He said, "It was wonderful. My whole body got tingly."

Then he lay there for probably an hour asking me how it feels to go through life alone, how it can be that I don't have anyone to kiss like that, and encouraging me to begin looking for a man I could enjoy that part of life with. He then told me something I will never forget. He said, "Mom, one day a man is going to come along and see every level of psycho that you are, and he is going to love you anyway, and I cannot wait to watch that happen."

I'm telling you, I've recalled those words every day, at least once, since the night he said them to me.

In November of 2014, when the owners of the home we had been renting decided to sell their property, we moved into an apartment and had to give the dog, Savannah, back to Chad until we could move into a pet-friendly place. Gabe was fully immersed in school, planning his college future and experiencing his first heartbreak. He was as stubborn as ever and continued arguing with his dad whenever they disagreed. He turned 18 that month and believed that he was a full-grown adult. He made choices that I disagreed with and used his newfound independence to disobey curfews and rules, and generally acted rebellious. He was working hard to establish his own identity in the world. I watched and tried to understand, but I had an unsettled feeling about his attitude, including the notion that he believed everything in moderation was OK—legal or illegal—and he wasn't going to waiver in his opinion.

I didn't know it at the time, but the other side of the hurricane was about to hit shore.

Chapter 4

The Worst Best Note

I - December 2014

The following winter, Gabe and his girlfriend were going through a breakup. I tried to tell him it would be the first of many heartbreaks that every person needs to endure, but he had a hard time understanding that. Ben was happily married, Luke was engaged to be married the next spring, and I think he believed he was next in line to have a committed relationship, even though he was so young.

To compound matters, he had anxiety about where he would be going to school the following year, and because of his part-time job and the college class he was taking, time was a precious commodity that he really didn't have enough of.

One night in late December, he told his dad that he was thinking about suicide. Chad told me and the other boys, instructed us to not leave him alone, and recommended setting up an appointment with a counselor he knew that he believed could help Gabe. We agreed to everything. I recall thinking that he was being a really good parent by being proactive in this way.

It was never unusual for Gabe and me to lie on the couch and talk or for me to go into his room and lie on his bed, looking at the ceiling and talking about life. During this time, we did that much more frequently, and I tried to talk to him about his thoughts on suicide. Every time I mentioned it, he'd say, "Mom, I'm not going to talk to you about this."

I never pushed the subject.

He went to the counselor a couple of times, but as far as I know most of the conversation was regarding symptoms of depression, excluding suicidal thoughts. He was having trouble sleeping, eating, and concentrating, and during his sessions I believe they discussed ways to help those symptoms.

For Christmas that year, all of my boys and their girls were home, and we went to my sister's house an hour north to celebrate with my side of the family. We enjoyed several days of togetherness, and I kept a close eye on Gabe, checking his mood frequently.

On the day after Christmas, he talked to his girlfriend on the phone. I don't know the exact conversation, but when they were finished, he called me from the basement of my sister's house (I was upstairs) and asked me to come down and be with him.

I opened the door to a storage area in their basement and found him sitting on the floor, sobbing. I grabbed some tissues and sat down next to him. That 18-year-old boy crawled into my lap and put his head against my chest, weeping and trying to explain that he really thought his girlfriend was breaking up with him forever. I tried to tell him that if it's meant to be, it will work itself out. He couldn't hear me. So I just held him.

He then told me that he felt like he was turning into his dad. He said, "Mom, I'm a mess. I'm just like him…I'm short on patience and mean to girls."

It was one of the most precious things I've ever heard another human say. I assured him that because of his intense humility, he was going to be fine. The fact that he could say how broken he was made me think that he knew he could work through this.

After we left my sister's house, the older boys spent a few days at their dad's, and Gabe and Jordan went with them. Each night, Gabe came home to my apartment so he could sleep in his own bed. For New Year's Eve, we watched *Forrest Gump* and ate pizza, just the two of us.

The first couple of weeks of January brought bitter cold and gray skies. Wisconsin winters do not include much sun, and the dreariness of the weather often brings me down; as we buckled in for a long winter, I wondered if the same would happen to Gabe.

I helped him begin applying to colleges he was interested in, and helped him practice for spring play tryouts, which were to take place during the third week of January. Because he was looking ahead to his future, I worried less and less about his depression, but his sleeping and eating habits still had not gotten back to normal.

II - Wednesday, January 14, 2015

Gabe worked at Taco Bell until 10:00 PM that night, not an unusual shift for him during the week. While he was working, Jordan told me that a friend of his saw Gabe at Walgreens the night before, buying sleeping pills. That worried us both, and after a short discussion, we decided to see if we could find them in Gabe's room so that we could get rid of them.

It didn't take much looking to find them, and I hid them in a dresser drawer, thinking that I was being a good mom by taking away any temptation that may come from those pills.

Gabe walked in at around 10:30 and immediately went to his room and shut the door. He came out a few minutes later and asked who was going through his stuff and where his sleeping pills were. I told him it was me. He asked how I knew about them and Jordan told him about his friend at the drugstore.

For the next two hours, I watched and listened while my child began to yell at me for being nosy, yell at Jordan for being a "rat," and threw all three of his brothers under the bus for shit they'd done while in high school. Gabe was acting so out of character that night, all I kept thinking was that he needed to go to the hospital. I told him I wanted to take him there. I told him all of his schoolwork would be excused. I told him they'd be able to help with his depression.

He fought me. He made it clear that he wouldn't go and that I needed to stop suggesting it. At one point in the argument, he even stated, "Mom. If I was going to kill myself, I'd just do it. I wouldn't need to take pills."

I realize now how crazy this sounds, but it actually gave me some peace inside, hearing him say this to me. It was like a reassurance of some kind that I didn't have anything to worry about, like he was telling me to calm the fuck down and to stop worrying about something so silly. So I dropped the subject and told both boys to go to bed; it was past midnight and we all needed some sleep.

At 3:00 AM I was still awake. Gabe's room was right next to mine in our apartment and I could see that his light was still on at that hour, so I peeked in and saw him lying on his bed studying. I walked over to him and rubbed his hair for a minute and told him to go to sleep. I knew he had a test the next day that he was worried about, but I wanted so much to see him get some sleep.

At 6:00 that morning, after I had managed about fifteen minutes of sleep, I called for a substitute teacher because I was in no condition to manage my class that day, and I went in to tell Gabe that I wanted him to stay home from school. I told him I'd call him in sick and he could just try to catch up on some sleep he'd been missing for days. He refused. I begged him but he argued that he had a test and all kinds of things to do that couldn't be made up, so I backed off.

Jordan and Gabe left for school and I tried to fall asleep. For reasons I really don't understand, I could not. I called our pastor, Russ, whom I hadn't seen in many months, and asked if I could spend some time with him that day talking. He agreed and we met that afternoon, and I told him everything.

My boys had reached a stage of rebelliousness and from all appearances, I had lost any ability to reach them through my own example, rules and efforts to talk with them about changing behavior. I did not know exactly how to handle their poor choices and blatant disobedience.

A year earlier, Gabe expressed some questions he had regarding the existence of God. He sat on the bottom step of the house we were living in while I sat next to him and he simply said, "Mom, I think I'm an atheist."

I asked why he thought that.

He said, "Who's the biggest hypocrite you know?"

I told him his dad was.

He said, "Exactly. He shoves the Bible down our throats and then hires a prostitute. He talks nonstop about how to be a Christian but he is the worst example of anyone I've ever met. It's hard for me to believe in a god that allows that."

I tried to understand what he was saying and I didn't try to talk him out of his feelings. In fact, I believe I told him that I was so proud that a 17-year-old would even think of things so profound. We had many discussions after that regarding how he felt, and I never agreed with him but I did validate why he may have felt that way. I only tried to use tangible examples of where I felt God could be seen: in the smiles and hearts of children who have nothing, in the vibrant colors of spring as earth comes back to life, and in the way he and his brothers were all so different, yet each one was raised with the same rules and the same love under the same roof. He never wavered from his argument, but I like to think that maybe I gave him some reasons to think more.

III – Thursday, January 15, 2015

I think the worst part of the divorce for the children was listening to their dad talk shit about me every time they were with him. They'd come home from a weekend with him and tell me that for four days, all they heard was how I divorced the family and that I was trying to destroy their relationship with him. Both boys tried, at the beginning, to correct him, but he would hear nothing of it. This continued even after the divorce was final, but the boys had gotten used to it, and I tried hard to not react when they'd come home and complain about it.

I decided on that January day that it might be best for them to begin a 50/50 placement split between my house and their dad's. I knew if we did, the negativity would end and the boys would not have to listen to it anymore—which would eliminate much of the stress in their lives. I also believed that perhaps Chad's rules for curfews and behavior might be obeyed, and I knew they both needed some self-discipline to try to get them back on track. I remember telling Gabe that afternoon when he came home from school and he responded, "Mom, you don't mean it."

I assured him that I did, and tried to convince him that it would end the battle we'd fought for over two years so he wouldn't have to listen to the negativity any more.

What I didn't know was that on that day in school, after only three hours of sleep, he found out that he didn't get a part in the school play (which was quite shocking, considering his commitment to the drama team at school as well as the fact that he'd landed a part in every other play he'd ever auditioned for), and he'd had a falling-out with his girlfriend. Their month-long breakup ended with that last fight.

Jordan had basketball that night, so Gabe and I ate some soup together and had some very tender conversation regarding life, love and choices. After dinner, I encouraged him to get ready for bed since he was so short on sleep, and I stood at the sink washing dishes.

He went to his room and I heard him talking on the phone. I found out later that he was talking to his dad, who was at the time with his girlfriend about a half hour away. Gabe came into the kitchen carrying his laundry basket and his backpack. I looked at him in a confused way and tilted my head a bit, asking where he was going.

He replied, "I'm going to Dad's."

I asked why.

He said, "I'll be more comfortable there."

Hindsight is 20/20. I think that may have been his cry for me to help him, and I didn't even know it. I just looked at him with bewilderment, because that was something he would never, not in a million years, say. I guess I thought at that moment that it was a diss. A jab. A way for him to say, "Ha...I'll show you..."

I asked, "When are you coming back home?"

He said, "You'll see me tomorrow, Mom."

Then he put his basket and backpack down and wrapped his arms around me. He gave me the longest hug he'd ever given me and then kissed me seven or eight times on my neck and cheek. I reciprocated. When I tried to release from the hug, he kept holding me; I chuckled a little sigh of joy at that and squeezed him extra tightly and said, "I love you so much, Gabe. So much."

He replied, "I love you too, Mom."

Then, he picked up his belongings and walked down the stairs. I heard him start the car and close the garage door, and I went back to washing the dishes.

About thirty minutes later, I got a text from Ben asking if Gabe was OK, because he just got a weird text message from him. I replied that he was at Dad's and wanted to know what the text said, but before he replied, I got another text, this time from Luke. He, too, wanted to know if Gabe was OK.

A moment later, Ben called and asked me to try to call Gabe because he tried but Gabe didn't answer. So we hung up and I tried to call, but no answer. Then Luke called and asked me to do the same thing. I tried again to call Gabe and I texted him, but no response came.

I called Ben and told him I was going to go to Dad's and I'd call as soon as I found Gabe. On the way to Chad's house, I called to ask him if Gabe had arrived yet, but he told me he was at his girlfriend's house and that Gabe was alone. I raced down Highway P on that dark and cold winter night with a sense of panic and determination.

Chad still lives in that large house he built on the six-acre lot. It is a large home, roughly 3,500 square feet, with a large detached garage that sits about fifty feet from the house. When I got there, the attached garage door was open, and I saw Gabe's car. Relief. I went in the house and called for him, but no answer came. I continued to call his name while I began looking in every room and closet and corner of that house, but I couldn't find him. I began to panic; I believe a mom instinctively knows when something isn't right. As I searched for him, I began to believe I might find what would be any parent's worst nightmare.

I called Chad again and he told me he was twenty minutes away. He said he was sending Eric (one of his employees) over to help me look. I told him I was going to call 911.

I dialed the emergency number while I was still looking all over the house. At one point, I left the house and went to the detached garage, where a light had been left on, and I stood at the door looking past the tractors and trailers that were parked in there, but I saw nothing. I don't remember a lot about the conversation with the dispatcher, but I do remember getting frustrated in my panic that she was asking me where I live and who lives in the house I was at. Finally, Eric pulled into the driveway just as I was coming out of the house again to begin looking around the yard.

He walked into the detached garage and came out a few seconds later, just as I was about to follow him in there. He grabbed me by my arms and shouted, "Don't go in there, Bonnie!"

I yanked my arms out of his hands and said something to the effect of "Get your hands off me," and I walked in. This time I didn't stop at the doorway but walked to the end, past a flatbed trailer, and I saw him.

Lying on the floor, legs slightly bent, one hand by his side and the other resting on his right leg, was my boy. His eyes were closed and his lips were shut. Under his head was a pool of blood. In his chin was a hole, about the size of a half-dollar. Lying on the trailer next to him was a shotgun, the very one I begged my ex-husband not to buy several years ago. I fell to my knees and lay down on his legs and held his hand.

It was still warm.

I don't know how long I stayed there, lying with him. I only know that while I lay there I felt close to him and I didn't want to leave his side. I think I probably knew he was dead, but I remember thinking I just wanted to lie there with him while he slept.

At some point that night, I learned months later, several officers came in but I don't remember seeing any of them. I only remember my friend Alex, a deputy, coming in and telling me it was time for me to go. I believe he picked me up and helped me get into the house.

I wish now that I had thought about taking some of Gabe's hair.

Jordan was at a basketball game about an hour away that night. I didn't go because he wasn't going to play. Alex took his squad car and picked him up from the high school; Jordan knew something bad was going on because during the ride home on the bus, kids were asking him if Gabe was missing—I guess someone posted something on Facebook about people looking for him. He also read a text message that Gabe had sent him. I found out later that Gabe had sent a message to his former girlfriend that evening. When she tried to call and he didn't answer, she began calling their mutual friends.

Jordan was told to stay on the bus while the other players got off. Alex walked onto the bus and told him something bad had happened at his dad's house and that he would take him there. Jordan told me later that while driving to his dad's house in a squad car with the lights and sirens on, he thought he already knew. We don't talk about that ride. We had one conversation about it because I needed to know everything; I honestly cannot imagine the thoughts that were going through his mind, and I'm guessing that on his darker days, he must fight the recollections and feelings he had at that moment.

When Jordan walked into the house, he looked at me. I didn't have to say anything. He knew.

He wrapped his arms around me and began to cry; by this time Chad had gotten home and was screaming and breaking stuff all over the house. Russ had been called, as had our friends Tim and Lisa, and we all sat at the kitchen table, while they decided how to tell Ben and Luke. I recall them asking who was going to tell them, and since Chad stated that he couldn't, I had to.

Russ set up a group call and when they were both on the phone, I remember not being able to say the words. I fumbled for a while and then Russ took my arm and told me I had to tell them.

I only said, "Gabe isn't with us anymore."

Luke wailed. Ben was furious. I recall him telling me he was at the gym and all he wanted to do was smash the television. He kept saying "fuck." Luke kept wailing. Jordan leaned on my arm. I sat there in shock, unable to cry, unable to feel. I gave instructions to both Ben and Luke, telling them how to get home. The coroner came in and started talking to me about donor gifts. I signed the papers for Gabe.

Some EMTs came in at some point, and I remember just looking at them and wondering why the hell they weren't tending to my child—I felt confusion and rage at that moment, wondering where Gabe was and thinking that they needed to be taking him to the hospital. Nothing made any sense.

They asked if I was OK. I just stared at them.

Tim and Alex helped Jordan and me get back to my house. I closed the garage door, Jordan and I walked up the stairs, and at the top of the stairs we both paused, looked at each other, and then the tears came.

After spending some time holding Jordan in my bed, he fell asleep. I did not. I wandered around the apartment most of the night in the dark, wondering what just happened. I went onto the deck and smoked a cigarette at some point, and there were people having a party in an apartment across from ours. I sat there thinking, "They're having a party. How can they be so happy? Don't they know that Gabe has died?"

Several times during that night I curled up next to Jordan in my bed and put my hand on his head. I felt his warmth. I listened to him breathe. I remember thinking, "He's still alive. I have to keep him alive." I remember going into Gabe's room many times, looking for him; I also recall sitting on the edge of the couch looking out the window, waiting for his red car to pull around the corner. I would sit on the edge of the couch like that for the next two months, smelling his shoes and waiting for him to walk up the stairs.

IV - January 2015

The first few days after he died are a combination of crystal-clear images mixed with blurriness. I can remember locking on to images like the calming look on his face when he said, "You'll see me tomorrow," or walking into the detached garage and seeing his feet lying next to the end of the trailer just before I saw the rest of his body. Those things are still so clear, it's as though I'm looking at them right now, but I also know that at times, when people talk about those early days, I have no recollection of what they're talking about.

Food was being brought to us and all I could wonder was who would eat it. People came, people called, text messages were coming in, and I have no idea if I talked or replied to anyone.

I do remember the moment that Luke and Anne walked in, as well as the moment Ben and Martha did. I realized upon looking into their eyes that no words were adequate; nothing needed to be said, so nothing was. We only embraced.

I did go find every photo of Gabe I owned and laid them all out in the family room. I got his teddy bear and blanket and didn't let go of them for many days. I still sleep with them every night.

My sister Karen came that morning. I know that I had called her in the middle of the night to tell her, asking her to let my dad and our other sister, Laura, know; I didn't want to talk to anyone, and I certainly didn't want to have to tell the story out loud. When she pulled up in front of the apartment, I went down the stairs and opened the door. She tilted her head and then pulled me into her. She understood. She knew me, she knew Gabe, she was a mom; she knew. I remember thinking, "I can't let her go. She needs to hold me together. Her life is going to change too."

On Friday night, Martha and Anne instructed me to take the Valium that had been prescribed for me. I agreed only because I could see the worry in my children's eyes and knew they were hoping I'd get some rest. I remember thinking that it wouldn't be so bad if I became a drug addict, as long as I was alive. I woke up the next morning unable to recall whether I'd had a nightmare or if Gabe had really died. When I looked in his room and saw my ex-husband sleeping in his bed, I knew it was real.

The tears came again.

That day, my children, pastor and ex-husband took me to the funeral home to make arrangements for his body and his service. We decided upon cremation and the funeral was set for Tuesday night, so as not to disrupt the school schedule. The district administrator had called the pastor to let him know that school would be cancelled if the service was during the day. I remember thinking, when Russ told me that, how much Gabe would love to get school cancelled for everyone. That would be a proud moment for him.

During the meeting with the funeral home director, I remember putting my head down on the table and Luke pulling me back up and saying, "Oh no, you're not going to do that." I was ready to give up and he knew it. He wasn't going to let that happen.

We went into a closed room to look at urns. I hated them all. I wanted to throw up, thinking how ugly they were and how there was no way my kid was going to live inside one of those.

I looked at photos with the kids. We had to choose some to go in a slideshow for the funeral. I got upset that they wouldn't let me use all of them.

We went to the cemetery to find a plot for his headstone and, wandering around the grass, I remember thinking, "I don't want him to be here." I held on to his favorite shoes and a photo book of his senior pictures.

I was nauseous at the smell or sight of food. I kept thinking how my only job was to protect my boy and I failed. All I could think was that if he couldn't eat, I wasn't going to either. It seemed so selfish.

We chose songs to go with a memorial video that someone was making for Gabe's service. Ben played the video on his phone while I sat next to him on the couch. I remember singing along to "You Are My Sunshine" and crying, then putting my head in his lap while he rubbed my hair and cried too. I recall thinking, "Well, now my boy is the parent and I'm the child. I hope he's OK with this."

Luke, desperate to see me eat, tried to feed me and I couldn't swallow anything. He was getting worried and begging me to eat anything and I kept thinking, "Well, now my kids are going to watch me disintegrate into nothing. I hope they eat anyway."

Jordan woke up several times in the middle of the night after a nightmare. After I was done comforting him, he'd have to comfort me. I remember thinking, "Well, I guess he lost his mom and his brother at the same time."

I watched Luke and Ben care for Jordan during those early days while Anne and Martha cared for me. I kept wondering what was going to happen when they all left the two of us alone, thinking how inadequate I was as a mom and wondering if it would be best to have Jordan move in with one of his brothers.

I was told that the coroner would be doing an autopsy. I began to have images of my child's body being cut up and destroyed with a scalpel, and the image of it seemed so real and so ugly that it consumed me for weeks. I had given birth to a perfect, beautiful boy and he had grown into a perfect, beautiful young man, and yet in minutes they were going to mutilate him. With each cut of the knife, I imagined him lying there screaming in pain but unable to make any noise, and I stayed in my apartment and did nothing to stop any of it. The imaginary layers of horror that were emerging in my head began to take over my reality... I could see the coroner standing over him in a cold, sterile room with blood covering his white coat. I could see his body being pushed into the fire to be burned. I could see his organs being removed and placed into a cooler. And I could see his last moments...the look on his face...the anguish in his eyes...

But I couldn't feel what he felt. That's what got me the angriest—I had no ability to understand what his last thought was before he decided to pull the trigger. I kept imagining that he said to himself, "Just pull the fucking trigger," and then he did. At times, I imagined that he calmly took the gun to the garage and without any hesitation, just pulled the trigger. The worst that I imagined was that he stood there with the gun against his chin and waited for me to show up and save him. That he was crying out, "I don't want to do this... Mom, where are you? Come quickly..." And I didn't come.

I didn't come.

Through the course of the week they were there, the girls, along with my sister and Russ, took care of all of the details. Chad had moved into my apartment for that week at the request of Ben and Luke so he could be close to us. At some point I recall him saying to the kids, "Do you see what divorce can do?" I didn't have the energy to respond, but I knew enough to tell myself that divorce does not cause death.

Eight hundred fifty people came to his funeral. Jordan said, days later, "I think if people could look ahead to their funeral they would make different choices in their lives."

My memories of the day of his funeral are still blurry; I do know that I had several students who came, and I did not want them to see me in the condition I was really in, so I did my best to hold myself together. Residual effects of the Valium I was still taking at the request of my children caused me to be stuck in my own purgatory. I was told later that I was in shock during those early days. It caused me to waver somewhere between staring ahead, expressionless, and weeping uncontrollably while my lifeless body struggled to even hold on to a Kleenex. At the funeral, Ben sat on one side of me with his arm around me, Jordan sat on the other side with my arm around him.

I managed to write a eulogy for the pastor to read. It can be summed up in my description of him as a boy who would never conform, and as a young man who loved fiercely and with so much passion that it could never be contained. I reminded the attendees that what he did does not define his life; I asked them to remember the living Gabe.

Ben and Jordan had written something for him to read as well, and Luke got up and spoke. I recall, listening to the words spoken by them all, thinking how simple and precious the love they all felt for one another was. Listening to stories of passing gas, practical jokes and childhood arguments was refreshing; I knew these were things none of them would ever forget. At one point in his tribute, Luke even said "damn," then quickly added how proud Gabe would have been that he just cussed in church. Roars of laughter filled the sanctuary; these people were learning my child.

A few days after the funeral, shortly before the older kids had to go back to their lives, their concern was great. They needed some kind of reassurance that I was going to be all right, and I had no ability to give it to them. So they took matters into their own hands. Anne made me go on a short walk with her. Martha, Ben and Luke drove me to the bank and Ben walked in with me. We ran into a woman who cornered me and began asking questions like, "Why would Gabe do that? My son keeps asking me why and I don't know what to say. Did you have any signs he would do this?" With each syllable she spoke I began to feel myself getting weaker; Ben could see it too. He took my arm, pulled me in and calmly walked me back out to the car, and he said, "Mom, people are going to be stupid. They won't mean to be, but they can't help it." I believe that maybe it helped them all stay patient during the following months when I was too scared to go anywhere.

I went home that night and fell back apart. Later in the week after everyone except Jordan had left to go back to their lives, shit got real.

I was suicidal in a big way.

The only thing I wanted was to hug my child; everything else seemed trivial and meaningless. The idea that I would never again hold my child was inconceivable, and with every passing day, I felt like I was getting farther away from him instead of closer to the time I'd see him again. Nothing made sense regarding time; it was like the day he died, my entire life got split into a "before" and "after." I liked the "before" part; he was with me. I wanted to go back to before. And his hand...it was still warm... I came too late. Minutes too late. I somehow thought if I could go back, even if everything else was the same, if I had just come a few minutes earlier, he would still be alive. I could have stopped him.

I wanted to go back to the before. In my delusional state, I believed somehow that I could, but I didn't know how, and so with each passing day I began to feel anger.

I mentioned to Jordan at one point that first week without his brothers there that I wanted to smash something. He told me he did too.

I told my friend Alex about it and he had us come over to tear down a bathroom in his house he was getting ready to remodel.

We walked in and his wife gave us each a mask. Alex handed us a sledgehammer. They left and went to a different part of the house.

I swung first. I hit a few tiles. I gave the sledgehammer to Jordan. He did the same and then handed it back to me.

Something got into me and I started swinging it and knocking down dozens of tiles. I began cursing and screaming and crying and knocking down more tiles in a back-and-forth motion, so fast and with such power that I didn't even know I had in me. I hit the water line and cold water started pouring out of the shower onto me, and I fell to the floor, holding on to the sledgehammer, and just started wailing.

I cried for my boy. I cried for my other kids. I cried for myself. I cried for every human he ever knew and for all of us who, if we could, would do anything to bring him back.

And then, as quickly as it happened, I was done.

Jordan and Alex helped me get up and we left. On the way home I told Jordan, "I'm sorry you didn't get to smash stuff."

He said, "It's OK, Mom. I didn't need to; I took you because I knew you did."

V – February 2015

Jordan went back to school and was given leniency on his schoolwork and tests, and was told he could text or call me at any time during the day. He bravely stepped back into his life.

I did not.

I couldn't go back to work. Hell…I couldn't leave the apartment. I couldn't eat. I couldn't sleep. I could think of nothing except the last twenty-four hours of Gabe's life; I was in some delusional state that looped those hours over and over. I kept searching for the door or the clue that would allow me to go back and change the outcome.

This went on for at least a month.

At one point I was down to 110 pounds and decided I'd go to the post office. I ran into someone I knew who looked at me, smiled, and said, "Bonnie, you look really good," and I recall looking at her in a state of confusion mixed with rage and thinking, "What the fuck is wrong with you? Really good? I look really good? I just lost my baby and you're going to tell me I look good?"

I remember sending snap chats to Gabe and watching my phone all day to see when he would open them, and then being confused when he didn't.

I would sit on his bed for hours and smell his shoes. I liked the scent. I did that a lot. And then, heartbreakingly, I realized the scent was fading.

I managed to write down my thoughts at that time, not knowing why but understanding that I needed to let something out; to communicate with the outside world since I had decided to seclude myself completely, even though others were reaching for me. I know my friends and acquaintances meant well, but their trite words frustrated me. This is an excerpt from a note I posted on Facebook:

The texts began last night, from well-meaning people asking if I'm going to church today. I went last week...stood in the back and watched as the congregation raised their arms and sang, "He makes all things work together for my good" and I lost my composure. I had another one of those breakdowns where it's hard to even breathe through the tears that stream down my face. I left. I came home and spent the rest of the day laying on my couch wondering how in the world the God I know can use the death of my child for His good. I'm having a hard time with that idea.

I have a friend to whom I write emails to release my thoughts without expecting a reply. We call it a purge; I began a letter to that friend this morning but decided it might be better to purge publicly today, for reasons I don't fully understand. I'm aware that my living children will read this, and I think that's ok. I'd rather be real than pretend to be someone I'm not, and I'm fairly certain I couldn't fake anything in front of them anyway, not to mention the understanding that the God I think I know sees the condition of my heart whether I say it out loud or not.

It's been 44 days since Gabe left us. In that time, we have received more love and support from this community than words will ever do justice to. For that, we are all most thankful. The financial support has paid for the funeral costs, the unending stream of meals has provided nourishment to us at a time when the simple act of preparing food seems like a monumental task, and the kind gestures of gift cards and words of encouragement have been received, as has the generous gift of a student's family who bought us airline tickets so my children and I can spend some time together during spring break. The following thoughts I have are indicative of the kindness shown to us all; please don't misinterpret what I'm about to say.

I'm a spiritual mess. Really. There have been moments in my life when I have questioned God's plan, His existence, and His power regarding good versus evil. Be honest—you have too. It's part of being human in an imperfect world. As I meandered down the path of divorce a few years back, my faith was challenged, yet I held tightly to the idea that God was with me and that He was carrying me and my boys through the storm. While I made some mistakes, I tried to live and set the example for Gabe and Jordan that **'integrity needs**

no defense.' If the most important job I have ever had is in raising my sons, the one thing I never want to give them is a reason to question my intentions. While I'm certain they have rolled their eyes on several occasions, I hold strongly to the belief that they know and understand my heart, and most importantly, I understand each of theirs.

What I can't seem to wrap my brain around, however, is the idea that the omnipotent God I thought I knew allowed my child to take his life. When I wake up at three in the morning and wander into Gabe's room, with some delusional sense that he will be sleeping in his bed and then realize that he's not, I sit on his bed and smell his shoes. I think the scent has begun to fade and yet I can still smell him. My favorite place to sit in my apartment is curled up in the corner of a love seat, where Gabe used to sit opposite of me, our feet touching, while we shared heartfelt conversations. The hallway from the door is parallel to my 'spot', and I sit there daily, waiting for him to walk in, carrying a Mountain Dew and a bean burrito from Taco Bell. He doesn't come, yet I continue to wait. I yearn to hear him say my name, to share a meal with him, to wake up and find dirty dishes in the sink from his midnight snack, and to spoon him and rub his soft blonde hair. I miss him being crabby in the morning and passing awful gas then blaming it on Jordan. I miss listening to him try to explain some complex scientific formula or mathematical equation to me while I sit there confused and then tell him he may as well be speaking Japanese before I kiss his neck and listen to him giggle. I miss him yelling at me for never stopping completely at a stop sign and him asking daily about my funny stories from school. I *miss him challenging my authority and asking me questions like how it feels to go through life without a partner. I miss hearing him say bad words and reminding me that I'm simple when I tell him to watch his mouth. I miss the special kind of hug that only he could give me—the kind where my head fits perfectly on his shoulder—the hug that was different than any other I've ever received. I miss my child, and no matter how much I ask, God isn't helping me with that.*

The Bible verses and prayers said for us and wishes that God will ease the pain...while it's probably all that can be done for us at this time, I'm just kind of pissed about the whole thing. It doesn't make sense to me at this moment how I can lean on God. In my mind, He allowed this to happen, and I'm just not sure how I'm supposed to honor a God that allows a brother (and best friend) to be ripped from the arms of my other babies and that allows a mother to both bring a precious soul into the world and then lay with him while he leaves. I don't expect an answer to that, by the way; it's a rhetorical thought, I suppose. Those of you who tell me we'll be stronger when we get through this—please stop. As far as I'm concerned, my kids were warriors before this happened. They didn't need this pain to make them stronger. I've been hearing since 2003 that I'm the strongest woman many people have known. Not sure how true that is, but even if only a fraction of it is, why would I need to become stronger through the death of my child? The truth is, I'm weak. Nothing you can say, no religious rhetoric or quote of encouragement is going to change that right now, and please—whatever you do—don't tell me that God only gives us what we can handle.

If that statement were true, He wouldn't have given this to us. Period.

I think reality is setting in. I'm realizing before I look in Gabe's room that he's probably not going to be there. He received his first college acceptance letter a week and a half ago. Arizona State University. He was awarded a $52,000 scholarship as well. When I got the letter, I looked up at the heavens and asked God what the hell, then I yelled at Gabe for not believing me when I would tell him of the brightness of his future. Then I was overcome with hurt because I wanted to have a celebration dinner with him and felt the stab of rejection in understanding that the dinner would not take place.

I can't explain why I'm writing all of this; at best, my mind is a cornucopia of thoughts and emotions. At worst, it is one simple word...

Why.

I guess at this point, I'm starting to understand that I won't have those answers until the day I hug my boy again; I can't say I'm alright with that idea, but I don't think I have a choice.

I guess it was my way of somehow trying to get everyone off my ass... I wanted to be left alone.

VI - March 2015

About six weeks after he died, my sister and boss decided they would try to encourage me to go to grief counseling. I wasn't working and had no idea if I could ever go back to school. My days at that point were mainly hiding in my apartment and listening to sad music and looking at

The Worst Best Note

photos every day, all day. I was nonfunctional and I didn't care. Food was being brought over so that Jordan could eat and I was dwindling away to nothing. I noticed that my hands were shaking nearly all the time. The only thing that seemed to help me relax a little was a bath, so I took a bath every day and put on a skullcap and yoga pants. I would call Ben on some days, and he would tell me a story about how Gabe was with God and how he was so relaxed and calm and happy. I don't know if I believed any of it at the time, but it always made me feel a little better to hear Ben tell the story. Sometimes now, I still long to hear his voice telling me about Gabe, but I don't burden him with it.

I watched my boys for signs of guilt and depression, even though now I know I likely would not have recognized either if they had been present; as each one went back into his own life, there were moments of discovery.

After Gabe died, Ben and Martha stayed for a week. Spring training was about to begin and he needed to go back to his life; we both understood that. That didn't make his leaving any easier, and I recall talking to him on the phone one night when I needed him to tell me the story of Gabe, when he told me, "Mom, I feel like I've abandoned you and Jordan."

At that moment, I realized the pain that my children were feeling was compounded by their desire to be present for each other and for me. I have told them all that I don't know how they feel… I didn't lose a brother and they didn't lose a son. So, the grief is different, yet so much the same. The memories choose us, the what-ifs and whys come when we least expect them to; all we have left is to hold one another up and remind each other of our unique importance in Gabe's life. When Ben said that—"I feel like I've abandoned you"—I had an unexpected reaction. I felt like it wasn't Ben, but Gabe, who abandoned us, and I (and likely *we*) honestly felt like we had abandoned Gabe. That was the first time I felt anger toward Gabe about what he did, and I had to process it. It was then that I understood the pain his action had caused my other children, his brothers.

Luke and Anne, newly engaged, were trying to plan their wedding. Amidst a time that should have been happy and full of hope, those two were grieving and trying to process an unfathomable loss. I didn't have a clue how to help either of them, but I found some peace in knowing that if they could get through this, they'd make it through anything.

Jordan, already a nonconventional student who couldn't learn the way his teachers wanted him to, used his time of grieving to become more rebellious than ever, and found offense in the trivial matters that his classmates and teachers thought were important. He became unafraid to say what he was thinking and at one point, punched a kid who made a derogatory comment about Gabe. I watched my child as he explained to me one night, after being caught racing a motorcycle 100 miles an hour down a country road, that he "has no joy in his life." It came to me that he had invested every bit of his relational energy into his friendship with Gabe for his entire seventeen years. That friendship had been ripped right out of his life. He was alone. He was hopeless. And I had no idea how to help him.

I only knew that the question, "What do we do now?" needed to change...it needed to become, "How do we keep Gabe alive?"

Over the next few weeks, while sitting in that desolate apartment, waiting on the couch for Gabe to come home, reality started to sink in.

One day, about two months after Gabe died, my boss and I decided it was time to come visit my class. I recall being scared of everything at that point in time (except death) but I reluctantly agreed.

Walking into the school, I saw the librarian and I grabbed her and started bawling. I wasn't sure I could go into my classroom. But I did. I walked into that classroom and my students got silent. They looked at me from their desks and I just stood there, thinking how beautiful they were and how they deserved better than to have me come in there like this, but the tears came anyway. At once, they all got up from their desks and surrounded me with a gigantic group hug. I touched every single one of them on their heads and said their names and then I left.

Shortly after that, one of my students' parents called my sister and told her she wanted to make a plan for me. My sister told her it wouldn't work, that I needed to make my own plan. When I found out about this conversation, all I could think was how I've never done anything right, and that I didn't even know how to grieve properly. Other people seemed to know what I should do, but I didn't have a clue.

My boys were touched deeply by the amount of community support we had. Between the food, the calls, the cards, the financial support and the general concern, they could see how loved we were. Between the divorce and Gabe's death, I am certain that my small town of highly empathic people felt a sense of helplessness at a time when they wanted to save us all, especially Gabe. I hold no angst against anyone, but I learned pretty quickly that people, filled with nothing but the best intentions, say things that can often make situations worse. People would tell me that God has a plan for everything, and I'd stare at them and wonder how I could have ever honored a God that planned this. People would say that God can turn everything into good and I'd shudder at the idea that any good could come from my child's death. People would tell me that he was with God, and it seemed so unfair; he should be here with me, I thought…he should be sleeping in his bed, making a mess in the kitchen, asking me for money. I know they were offering words of comfort, but in this situation, it all seemed like rhetoric to me, and it made things worse.

While I didn't want to leave the house, I had enough determination to not ruin my other children that I did attend Jordan's band concerts and basketball games. I usually went early enough so that I could find a spot to sit by myself, and I recall timidly looking up and hoping, as other people began to arrive, that no one would sit next to me. I became very observant. I remember feeling pissed every time a parent would get upset with her child, I remember thinking,

"Oh, if I could have Gabe back I'd never get upset with him again."

I remember watching other parents who knew Gabe and wondering how many of them understood that they could be me right now; that their child could be Gabe. I think every parent probably knew they could be walking in my shoes and not a single one of them knew what to do for me, but they all wanted to help.

My sister called one day and asked what I needed. I told her I didn't need anything, but "Jordan needs a new mom."

At one point, I found myself sobbing uncontrollably over the daughter-in-law I would never love. I mourned the grandchildren that I would never meet. I got mad at Gabe for taking those relationships away from me, and I shook my fists toward the heavens again and asked this so-called God why He would allow such intense love to disappear before it was even created.

I was a mess. I had no ambition. I looked like hell. I was angry. I was pushing people away. I looked back and remembered how broken I thought I was during the marriage. I realized that those years were a cakewalk compared to losing my precious Gabe. I wanted answers.

I had to ask myself over and over why it was that Gabe could be so distraught that he saw no other option in life than to end it.

And then, all at once, it came to me. I realized that it was not him or God that I was mad at; it was me. I was pissed at me. How could I have missed the signs? How did I not step outside of my own world and realize how he was really feeling? Had I loved him the wrong way?

I began viewing his death as some sort of punishment to myself for not being the kind of mom he needed me to be, and I took full responsibility in my mind for his death. I believed I had killed my own son.

I held on to these thoughts for a very long time; it was deserved punishment for me and it took all the responsibility away from Gabe. In my mind, it allowed him to remain perfect.

I cannot say at what point that passed—I only know now that it did. Sometimes I see graphs of the stages of grief that psychologists have put together and I think to myself what a bunch of bullshit that is. Grief is unorganized. It is messy. It is raw. It has no order and no timeline and absolutely no mercy. When I was able to come to terms with the idea that Gabe had his own mind and his own abilities, I gave myself grace for the way I parented him, and I began to see that he made a choice—a bad choice, but a choice nonetheless. How I would deal with it for the remainder of my days was completely up to me; his choice caused me to make my choice.

I wanted to know where he was. I remember feeling this intense sense of panic because I couldn't figure out where he was. I have read the Bible cover to cover, twice in my lifetime, yet the concept of him being on the other side was so ambiguous. I remember thinking that I'd have a better idea of where he was if I had sent him to a complete stranger's house and left him there.

At some point, I realized what was going on in my mind; the state of confusion I had could be summed up in this simply query: What was I going to do with all the love I wanted to give to Gabe?

VII – April 2015

It was during these weeks that I began to realize that I was stuck. I guess the best way to explain it is that I felt like I was in one of those snow globes, just sitting there watching the world go on, while I just took up space. I gave nothing and I received nothing. I began to understand that I left at the same time Gabe did. The only difference between his death and mine is where we both exist now.

Then I got pissed. I didn't know much, but I knew Gabe loved me. I knew he wanted to quit, but I also knew he didn't want me to. I began to understand that if he knew the condition I was in, he'd be so mad, and at that point, I understood that I needed to make a decision: I could choose life or I could choose death, but I couldn't sit in that snow globe any longer.

At that moment of discovery, I decided, based purely on the love I have for a child I can no longer show it to, as well as my undying love for my other children, that I would choose life. I knew that if I didn't, they would live the rest of their lives knowing their brother and their mom died on the same day. I was not going to let that happen.

I agreed to the grief counseling.

My principal, David, picked me up and drove me to Elkhorn. I sat down in Kim's office and she asked why I was there. I told her my child died by suicide. She said, "Tell me about Gabe."

So I did.

I told her I have four sons, three who look just like their dad and one who got all my genes. I showed her a picture of him.

I told her he was creative and bubbly and talented and likely the smartest person I had ever known. I told her he was sensitive and emotional. I told her that he and his dad never saw eye to eye. I told her that my other boys used to refer to him as my sidekick, because in many ways, he was. I told her that he protected me and encouraged me and pushed me to get outside of my comfort zone.

I told her he was going through his first heartbreak and that he was experimenting with pot and possibly other drugs. I told her that he used to sit with the kids in the cafeteria who didn't seem to have any friends, and his friends would ask why he was sitting with the misfits. I told her that he was taking college classes because his computer teachers didn't know what else they could teach him, and in those classes, he was helping the older college students with their projects.

I told her that one day, a few months earlier, he sat at his computer one Sunday, all afternoon, furiously trying to calculate something, while I would come and rub his shoulders and ask if he needed anything. When he'd try to explain what he was doing, I'd tilt my head as though he were speaking in a foreign language and he'd look at me with those gigantic blue eyes and smile, telling me I'm simple,

The Worst Best Note

and I'd just kiss his cheek. A little later, he erupted with a loud, "MOM! I DID IT!" When I asked what he did, he told me he calculated the mass of the sun. I recall looking at him with a huge smile and thinking how much I adored the fact that he was different than any human I'd ever known.

I told her that he had been struggling with depression and anxiety and his sleeping and eating habits had changed, and the only thing I knew to do was to love him. I told her how I used to lie in his bed and rub his hair. I told her how we used to sit on the couch and I'd listen to him cry and try to tell him that things would get better, that he just needed to hold on.

I told her that he gave up. I told her how I found him on that garage floor and I couldn't get that image out of my mind. The only job I had was to protect my child and I failed.

I failed.

And I told her that I wanted five more minutes with my boy.

I told her about the notes he wrote his brothers and that I didn't get a note, and I felt bad about that. I couldn't understand why.

You know what she said? She said, "Bonnie, you did get a note. You got the best one of all. You got the never-ending embrace and the kisses on the neck and the 'I love you Mom' that you'll hear every day, forever. Oh yes, you got a note all right."

That helped a little.

I told Kim that I wanted to be with him, but I knew that if I took my life too, it would destroy the other boys. I told her I would hang on.

I told her I was scared of everything, because I was. I told her I wasn't scared of death, though, because I wasn't. I'm still not. I've come to realize that any bereaved parent likely isn't. We know that on that day, we will finally hold our child again.

She told me Gabe was probably bipolar, with happy thoughts that turn rapidly into desperation; the racing thoughts are painful, she said, and the only escape he could think of was to die.

She told me that what the victims don't think about is the guilt the family members and friends will have to deal with their whole lives; Gabe probably thought about death as the only option and never considered what it would do to me or to his brothers. She explained that Gabe wouldn't want this to ruin my life and she promised me that if I made it through, I would find happiness again someday.

I can't say that I believed her.

She told me that he didn't want me to be the one to find him. She told me he did everything he could do to make sure I never saw him that night. I knew she was right about that.

One night, a few months after he died, my friend Alex and his wife Holly decided that they wanted to get me out of the house for a few hours. I was reluctant but they were relentless. So they picked me up and took me to dinner with one of their friends, Tommy.

The Worst Best Note

Two things happened that night.

In his studio after dinner, Tommy admitted to being suicidal most of his life. He told me he could understand why Gabe did what he did, and that if I do only one thing in the rest of my life, I needed to finish my book. He told me, regarding teaching (after I told him I felt inadequate to be responsible for an entire classroom full of children based on the fact that I couldn't even save my own boy), that he would undoubtedly rather have a teacher for his kids who had life experiences than some perfectly manicured human with unattainable expectations.

Tommy gave me life that night, even though I wouldn't realize it until many months later.

The other thing that happened was guilt. Guilt happened. The next morning, I woke up, looked in Gabe's room to see if he was there, and was overcome with a heaviness I'm certain I cannot describe. I had laughed the night before. I ate a full meal. I drank a beer. I was glad to be out of my apartment.

Shame on me. What kind of a mother goes out and does all of that while her child can't do anything? Who the fuck did I think I was?

That guilt lasted another three months while I vowed to myself that I would never again enjoy anything. I believed that I had dishonored Gabe by living, and nobody could have told me any differently. And so, while I began to work again and stopped at the gym each day to get a little exercise at the urging of Kim, I also got really good at finding ways to keep hiding.

And then one day, as quickly as the guilt came, it left. There was a moment of reality at some point during that summer, and again, I have no idea when it happened. I only knew that if I didn't get out and start to tell people about this boy that once lived, nobody would. I didn't have a choice anymore. I decided it was time to pull myself together.

Luke and Anne got married exactly four months after Gabe died. Gabe was to be one of the groomsmen. Because he was irreplaceable, Luke decided he'd rather have a space left where Gabe was to stand, and the bridesmaid who was to walk with him instead walked alone. Emotions were high on that day for everyone, especially me. I felt joy and hope; I was gaining another daughter-in-law and my son was marrying his soul mate. I hated that their engagement was spent grieving and yet I admired their strength and commitment to each other. Their vows were unique and perfectly written, and I'll never forget how Luke stood up there and told Anne that she inspired him. When the pastor announced that they were now husband and wife, Luke pulled Anne down the aisle and passionately kissed her behind all of the attendees. It was beautiful.

And it was awful.

It was the first of many life experiences that would not include Gabe. His void was more pronounced for me on that day, and I remember taking a photograph of the boys, their girls and myself and thinking, "This is my most recent family photograph." I looked at it and only saw one thing: Gabe wasn't there. The guilt I felt in thinking it was a family

The Worst Best Note

photo was crippling, until I studied that photo for days and suddenly it hit me: Gabe WAS there.

He was there all right. Every smile told the story: he was in our hearts and we all knew it.

During that summer, Jordan and I took a few trips to see his brothers and their wives. We took some bike rides. We went out for ice cream. He had his senior photos taken. We began to make plans for our future, even though it was hard to project; we somehow began to discover that we could survive, and the choice was ours to make as to whether we would live in the journey or let the journey rule us.

I found it very freeing to leave town during those summer months. While I was beginning to get out more, I also learned how to hide in my apartment while making it appear that I was not. I found our city to be rather suffocating, so when we went to different places, I realized that I could cry if I wanted, I could laugh if I wanted; nobody asked if I was OK and nobody tried to fix me. I liked how that felt.

Once school started in September, I was back in a routine exactly as I was in the spring, going to work, going to the gym, and hiding in my apartment. Sleep still didn't come easy, and somehow I was functioning most days on only a few hours of sleep. This caused me to be more emotional than a well-rested person, and I found that frequently I would still have breakdowns in front of my class.

They learned about Gabe. They learned about loss. They learned about life. I can't say they learned much in the way of ABCs and 123s, but maybe their lesson was bigger than that. All I know is that when twenty-four pairs of little eyes watched me while I wept, and they all ran to grab tissues for me so I could wipe my tears, it made a special place in my heart.

Once I realized I had some room in my heart for others, I also realized that they had love for me.

My only job was to receive it.

Chapter 5

Two Little Words

I – Fall 2015

For months after he died, I played the movie in my head of Gabe's last twenty-four hours. It would play through, beginning to end, then rewind and start all over. That movie played even while I was sleeping, and I woke up most often around three in the morning, usually opening my eyes and wondering if everything I was trying to process was actually a bad dream. I'd then get out of bed and go straight into Gabe's room to see if he was in his bed.

He never was.

Then I would pace through my apartment until dawn came and the realization hit me again that my boy was gone. Forever.

I realized that I couldn't move on with my life while repeating that pattern.

I now rent a house that Gabe has never seen. I cleaned his room at the apartment over the summer before I moved. All of his belongings are now boxed up in the basement of this home, with the exception of his baby blanket and his teddy bear, Cuddles, both of which (as I mentioned earlier) sleep in my arms every night. I was able to get Savannah back when I moved to the new house; it was a comforting trade for the heartache I felt, knowing I would no longer be able to go into Gabe's room and sit on his bed.

This year, just before the one-year anniversary of his death, I had a dream. It was beautiful. Gabe and I were at a party of some kind and he spent the whole evening talking with me and he had his arm around me, and I remember looking into his blue eyes and thinking how happy he seemed. I woke up and felt like I had been given the greatest gift…he visited me to tell me he was all right.

He only visited me one other night after that time.

One night I stayed home and made cookies. I took Savannah on a long walk. I texted a couple of friends. When Savannah and I were testing the cookies, I remember thinking, "Gabe would love these."

When I lay down in my bed, I looked at some photos of my kids all together, seeing their smiles and remembering some happy times.

I checked Facebook. I saw a cartoon of a hippo hiding under a bed with his blanket, and the memory of Gabe, probably when he was three or four years old, hiding under the bed with his bag of Halloween candy and happily eating it, flashed through my mind. It made me smile and broke my heart all at the same time.

I reread a text from a friend who went shopping for hunting ammunition and told me that he locked it up.

I held Cuddles and Blankie a little tighter and I closed my eyes.

I woke up the next morning, sideways on my bed, not sure where I was, replaying a dream I had.

What I recall from the dream is that Gabe was standing by a table full of guns and bullets. He was telling me how scared he was when he chose the gun he would use. I asked him why. He told me it was because he wasn't sure he'd recover from the wound.

I spent the first five hours of that day completely nonfunctional except to change the cover photo on my Facebook page to one of all four boys from a few years ago, laughing together.

I love that he visited me and told me how he felt, but what he said to me is excruciating.

I have often wondered what his final thoughts were on that cold night. I have made up so many fictional conversations I think he could've had with himself that I could fill a hundred pages with them, yet I never imagined he'd say what he did to me that night.

Not long ago, I attended a funeral for one of Jordan's friends. He died by suicide. I sat in the back pew of the church and couldn't stop looking at the mother (whom I don't know). I kept thinking that she and I are in a club together, and neither one of us signed up to be a member. We both want out, too.

I saw notes of sympathy on an online obituary and messages on Facebook to her, telling her to "let me know" if she needs anything, and it pissed me off so bad. Here's what I have learned from being in this wretched club: this mom doesn't know what she needs. She won't know for a long time. She'll be lucky to take in a few hundred calories a day and have the strength to shower once in a while. She'll hear people telling her, "Think about your living children" and "You need to move on" and "Be thankful for what you have left"—and it'll all make her feel worse than she already does, because she'll question her ability to even grieve properly.

Suicide leaves questions in the minds of every loved one left behind. No doubt about that. But for a mom, it's compounded. When a child is given to a mother, she knows that her job is to protect that being. The infinite love she feels for her baby causes her to do everything she can to protect him or her. So when she loses a child to suicide, the guilt is paralyzing. She plays the what-ifs over and over and over in her head until there are no more left, and then, more appear in her head.

She is consumed with the fact that she failed at the most important job she would ever be given.

She failed.

So looking at that mother, I couldn't help but project what her next few months will be like. The offers to help if she lets others know what she needs are ridiculous. It is not the job of a hurting person to reach out for help. It's like people are offering help they really aren't ready to give, just to make themselves feel better. Humans are funny that way…so quick to say they'll do whatever is needed, but not really ready to do anything. They only know they want to try to fix the situation.

If you remember only one thing from the thousands of words I write, please let it be this: **Some things cannot be fixed; they can only be carried.**

Some of us are unlucky enough to learn by default who our real friends are. They're the ones who aren't afraid to roll up their sleeves and get messy while trying to carry the pain. They're the ones who don't take offense when we say, "Leave me alone." They leave us alone but they don't go away.

Listen to me. A grieving mom is scary. Fuck…we scare ourselves. We're mad, in shock, in physical pain, heartbroken, lost, sad. We have nothing to offer and honestly, we don't want to receive anything either.

We only want our child back. That's it.

I think there's a strong possibility that people actually know all of that, which makes those offers to help seem hollow.

They're only hollow if they're not genuine. I recall talking to my sister one day; she asked me again what I needed and I told her I got my period and I had no tampons and no intention to go to Walmart and get some. An hour later, my doorbell rang. When I went to the door, nobody was there, but a box of tampons was hanging on my doorknob. I have no idea who brought them, but I do know they loved me. I began receiving gift cards in the mail, inside short greeting cards that simply said, "I'm thinking about you" or "You are loved." No signature, no return address, no pressure to write a thank-you note. It was genuine help coming from a genuine heart; the fact that recognition for it wasn't necessary made the gesture far more powerful, because it proved that someone really did care.

If you really, REALLY want to help, say her son's name. Ask her to tell you a story about him. I am telling you, that will make her heart sing. And she will regain hope. That's helping.

II – November 2016

Last week, while I was working at the bar, a young man came in. I hadn't seen him before so I asked for his ID. When he showed me, he said, "You'll recognize the name." I didn't, but I did notice that he was born in the same year as my second-born, so I asked him if he knew Luke.

He said, "Is that Gavin's brother? The one who shot himself?"

I looked that boy square in the eyes and I said, "His name is Gabe, and that's my son, and he may have shot himself but that's not all he did." Then I turned around and inhaled with the determination that I was not going to cry. Not there.

Parenting is the most rewarding yet thankless job any of us is ever given. No question about that. For bereaved parents, the burden lies in trying to keep their child's memory alive.

I know, without a doubt, that my child is alive and well inside my heart. Few thoughts in the day pass through my mind where I don't consider how Gabe would feel or react in a given situation, so that's not a burden.

The task at hand is to get the rest of humanity to understand that even though his life was short, he was here. He mattered. He loved. He existed.

Your avoidance in saying his name or your recollection of the night he died only exacerbates the heartbreak I feel, and I am 100 percent certain any grieving parent would tell you the same. Ask me to tell you a story about Gabe. Tell me he was beautiful. Mention his name when you talk about my other children, because he is still one of them.

Two months after Gabe died, Jordan had to have surgery to repair a broken collarbone. Just as he was going under the anesthesia, the doctor asked him how many brothers he had.

Jordan said, "Two."

He woke up in a panic, crying for the nurses to come get me so that he could tell me the guilt he felt. He asked me to explain to the doctor about Gabe.

I think people, in their attempts to be sensitive, avoid difficult conversations because it is easier. I realized on that day that Jordan, grieving his brother and best friend, had been programmed to do the same. While it was honorable to the doctors and surgical staff to not bring up Gabe's name at that time, what he learned was that it was not honoring to Gabe or to the relationship they shared. He has never again told anyone he has two brothers. The looks people give us when we explain that we lost Gabe tells us that they're sorry, but every time we mention him, we help to keep him here, with us, and we remind ourselves what an irreplaceable part of our lives he was.

I mentioned earlier that my spiritual condition had been compromised toward the end of my marriage, mostly, I think, because of the hypocrisy I was witnessing in Chad. I realize that God was not to blame for his behavior, but because of the way he seemed to be able to talk out of both sides of his mouth, I became confused.

Once I had met with Pastor Russ, I understood that perhaps God, in His omnipotent presence, was weeping right along with me. He understood how I felt and He was disappointed in the choices Chad was making. Because of that knowledge, I believed that He was with me through every stage of the divorce. With each passing court date and a favorable outcome for me and the kids, I believed we were being cared for and watched over by the one who created us, reminding me that He had my back.

When Gabe died, everything changed. My soul died too. I kept asking God what I had done to deserve the kind of pain that I was feeling, and I was furious that my children, who asked for none of this, had to suffer through such turmoil.

I wanted to know why this all-knowing, all-powerful being who could supposedly move mountains didn't help my child. I wanted to know why he didn't help *me* help my child.

It was beyond my ability to understand why, if the God I knew was so powerful, He allowed this to happen. I had nothing but questions…why wasn't the gun locked, why did Gabe know where the bullets were, why did his counselor not hospitalize him, why was he hopeless? I asked these questions while I shook my fists and yelled at this God that I honestly was ashamed to say I had ever loved.

I was in a fight with God that started the night I lay with my dead child.

Immediately following his death, I was inundated with advice and clichés from well-meaning people, telling me all the ways that God would make this good. I didn't know much, but I knew that if any of those sayings were true, I was never going to honor a god that works that way. No mother in this world can believe there is any reason her child should die before she does.

Their words made me feel worse because it minimized the grief, and when I found myself getting pissed off about what seemed like trite words spoken by others just because they didn't know what else to say, I felt even more alone than I already was. It made me think that maybe I was over-reacting, that because their words didn't make me feel better, there must be something wrong with my heart.

I didn't want to feel better. I wanted Gabe. And since I couldn't have him, I needed time to cry and wail and mourn and suffer and die, because in some unexplainable way, that was how I honored him. It was how I recognized both his life and his death.

So this fight with God I was having—it didn't make sense to the people who wanted to help. They thought I was making things worse by harboring anger toward Him, so they said the things they'd been conditioned to say in an attempt to help me.

I didn't pretend to have any spiritual beliefs and I certainly didn't believe I was going to get any answers, even though I know I told God I wanted them and I wanted them now.

My boys and daughters-in-law knew my condition, and while I'm certain they couldn't understand, I know they tried to.

Luke and Ben kept reminding me that we all have free will; if God had made us to be obedient, there would never be any hurt in the world. Anne, Martha and my sister validated my feelings by telling me that even though people say something good will come of this, there's nothing good about losing Gabe.

Jordan got a front row ticket to watch my unanswered questions turn into rebelliousness and anger, and I let it all happen because I didn't have the energy to try to save myself. On some level, I believe I was challenging God to just "bring on" whatever He was going to do to us next; I was standing in the boxing ring with my palms up, motioning my fingers as if to say, "Come on, big man, what else you got?"

Writing this now, over two years after his death, there are still days when the darkness rolls in like fog. I rarely see it coming ahead of time and I've learned that it's best to just let it consume me. I can't get off of my couch; I need to cry and remember and forget and relive and let go. And during those days, when the tears won't stop, I recall what Kim said to me about crying. During one session when I told her why I couldn't leave my apartment (because I never knew when the crying would start and people generally feel uncomfortable with watching someone cry) she told me, "Bonnie, every single tear you shed for Gabe brings honor to his life. You cry. Cry as much as you want to. His life mattered and the tears you shed for him proves that. Cry, cry, cry."

During one particularly crippling episode of grief I told my sister, "I just miss my baby. I want to touch him so badly. I need to hear his voice...forever seems like a really long time..."

Her response, authentic and heartfelt, gave me the first bit of peace I needed to begin true healing. She only said two words, but they are two of the most powerful words that have ever been spoken to me.

She said, "I know."

At a time when everyone else I had any contact with was trying to take my hand to help me up, my sister just let me be. She said, "I know." It would be the first time I thought that perhaps God knew too. That maybe He was somewhere just letting me be; that maybe, just maybe, I wasn't getting answers because He had none. Maybe He, as the divine creator, felt just as badly about Gabe leaving this earth as I did.

Two Little Words

On some level, I began to understand that in the same way He may have cried with me through the divorce, He may have wept the night Gabe took his life.

I began to picture Gabe, standing with his gigantic and hopeful blue eyes curiously looking at the Lord, whose arms were open wide and ready to embrace, but with a tear streaming down His cheek while He simply said, "Oh Gabe, what have you done?"

Shortly after Gabe's death, a friend gave me a jar that read "Pennies from Heaven." I didn't believe her when she told me to watch for pennies in strange places—that they would be messages from Gabe. That jar sat empty until that first November, when his birthday came and I was in a store with Jordan; we were wandering aimlessly around that day and at one point we stopped, looked down and saw a penny right between my feet. We both knew what it meant and that penny went straight to my jar. I began to find pennies in places where there was no explanation other than the idea that Gabe dropped one…on the seat of my car, inside a book cover that was on Gabe's nightstand, in the middle of a freshly vacuumed rug at the gym, at the bottom of my lunch box I took to school. Each time I find a penny, I stop and reflect and think of whatever it is that Gabe is trying to tell me. I listen. I remember through a small piece of copper that my child is here. I can't see him and I can't hear him and I can't touch him, but he's here and in a very big way.

III – Winter 2016

I don't go to church anymore at all. Instead of studying the Bible and singing songs of worship, I look at photos of my baby. I watch videos of him singing and I reread cards and letters he wrote to me when he was a child. I remember his voice, I feel his hug, I see his smile.

That's when I feel closest to God; that's when I know He is real. The messy, torturous hurt has turned into fond memories of the child named after an angel. While I wouldn't wish this pain upon anyone, I can say with absolute certainty that I'd rather carry the pain than to have never loved the child at all. The memories are my gift.

I recently read a question posed on a blog for bereaved mothers, asking what the hardest part of losing a child is. I read the question several times as I tried to compare one "hardest" part to another, when it occurred to me that there is no hardest part. That question is unfair. There is no hardest part because everything is different. Literally everything. You don't look at anything the way you used to. For a long time, nothing has meaning. You go through the motions of life for sheer survival purposes, but you are only depleting oxygen from the planet and nothing more. Then one day you realize that you left at the same time your child did, but you went to different places. It is at that moment of discovery that you either choose life or you choose death. Then, just like a toddler, you begin the process of discovering who you are, based mainly on the love you have for a child you can no longer show it to. It is tragic and heartbreaking and messy, and there's a hole in the heart of every mother that question is posed to. That hole, though—it has immense power—we get to choose how we use it, to either breathe life into the world or to suck it dry. It's a certainty that every bereaved mother has done both. The question—what is the hardest part—cannot be answered, because the woman before exists no more.

She exists no more.

The things I used to believe were important have no meaning anymore; the trivial matters that used to get me uptight seem so petty and meaningless in the whole picture of life. This experience has made me fierce. I have no time for small talk or bullshit because now I know this truth: **in one second, everything can change**. I am on a mission to love with a capacity so big it could never be measured, and I have the same intensity when it comes to intolerance for cruelty. I look at people from the inside out and I try to find one reason—at least one—to validate why they're here but my child isn't. Every single decision I make, because I knew my child better than anyone else, is based upon what he would have me do. I take offense to hurtful words and people who waste their lives being selfish and I try, with every ounce of energy I have, to be the difference in the world that my child needed but didn't get. I live with the motto that it's much easier to love than it is to hate.

And then I fall down. I smell his favorite food, I hear a song he loved, I remember a time when I got angry at him, and that fierce woman becomes a train-wreck all over again, weeping uncontrollably and angrily cursing the God that allowed my child to leave this earth before I did.

I retreat into the snow globe.

When I come out, I repeat the cycle. It is exhausting and exhilarating all at the same time, for reasons only those unlucky enough to know exactly what I'm talking about can understand.

In the end, I believe it's fair to say this cycle will only stop on the day I get to hug my child again, and while many may say that's not much of an existence, I beg to differ. It is the fierce woman and her fierce love that picks up the fallen-down woman and pulls her out of her snow globe; it is the love she has given to and received from her child, now on the other side, that fuels both of them. It is the tear, streaming down the maker's face, which reminds all three of them that in this life, there is only one thing that comes with a guarantee to last forever:

love.

Chapter 6

Pennies From Heaven

I – December 2016

Life, I have discovered, does go on. In what capacity, we each get to choose. One day, a few weeks after Luke and Anne were married, I was in the car alone with him. He said to me, "Mom, what do you want out of life?"

I said, "Hmm...well, I'd like to get Savannah back, I want to do more pottery, and I'd like to have my own garden."

He said, "How about a human? Did you ever think about that, Mom? You know, my brothers and I want nothing more for you than to see you be loved by someone. We need that."

Ouch.

Nope, I hadn't considered that in a long time.

Most of my adult life, I was attracted to bad boys. I've tried to psychoanalyze why, and all I keep coming up with is the idea that on some level, I believed that if I could get a bad boy to love me, I must have been more than just cute.

After the divorce, I didn't date for an entire year, despite the urging of my girlfriends. I think I knew that I couldn't introduce my train-wreck of a life to a man who was ready for love. I knew I wasn't ready and I didn't push the issue. I figured that I'd know when I was ready.

Shortly after Ben and Martha got married, I woke up one day and thought, "I'd like to have dinner with a man."

So I went with it. I created an online profile on Match.com and began looking for possible suitors. By the time I was ready to date, I had created a list of deal breakers and deal makers in my head so that I had something to go by, and also because given my experience being married to a bad boy, I knew I couldn't get myself into a relationship with a man like that ever again.

I began dating pretty quickly and learned even more quickly that the word of the day in dating online is "misrepresentation."

Even though I had used current pictures and been truthful in the process of describing who I was, that didn't seem to be the case with the men I agreed to go out with.

My very first date was arranged and we were to meet in a restaurant in Madison. Upon entering the establishment, I looked around for the guy I thought I made a date with. A heavy-set bald man began furiously waving at me, signaling me to a table. I had made a date with a fit man that had short brown hair, so I wasn't sure what was going on, but I walked to the table anyway, and proceeded to find out that the photos he used were from ten years ago. I sat there wondering why I even stayed, since his first interaction with me was actually based upon a lie, but I did. After dinner, which was both our first and last date, I realized I would need to ask men if their photos were current.

On another date with a man whose teeth were in such bad shape that I found myself looking away when he smiled, I learned that if they don't show photos with their mouth open, there's likely a reason.

Another gentleman, during a discussion on what we believe a whole relationship looks like, told me that he "doesn't allow any talking in my bed." At that, I excused myself to go to the bathroom and exited out the back door instead, wondering how long it would take him to realize I wasn't coming back to the table.

One man that I was hopeful of told me at the end of the date, "You're scary." I asked why. He said, "You're pretty, well spoken, educated and driven, and clearly you have some life experiences. Men won't know what to do with you." Then he asked me if I wanted to go kayaking. I declined and sat there wondering if men really only want a woman who'll get them a sandwich and then give them a blow job. I wondered if perhaps I was meant to simply be alone.

After Gabe died, I didn't date at all. In fact, I believe that I subconsciously vowed to just be alone forever; that if my boy would never experience love then why should I, not to mention the idea that I couldn't imagine any man ever being able to understand the real condition of my heart, and there was no way I was going to share the details of my precious child's life with someone who likely didn't deserve to know them.

But hearing my child, the intuitive one who never fills the air with fluff, say "We need that," that humans need love, I was at a loss. I didn't know what to say. I only knew that if there were someone out there for me, he'd have to find me, because I wasn't going to look for him.

For the first ten months of 2015, I pretty much spent my time hiding when I wasn't at work. While Jordan and I did some traveling to see my other children when we could, I found that my small town was a bit suffocating. I couldn't so much as even go to Walmart without running into someone I knew. That never bothered me until I was grieving; I felt like everyone was looking at me as if to say, "Oh, you poor woman," and I didn't like how that felt.

In November, shortly after Gabe's birthday, I attended an in-service meeting with other teachers from the district. A friend sat by me and while we were chatting about life, she asked me if I was interested in working as a bartender at the place where she works. I expressed some interest, mainly because I needed the money but also because I knew that a part-time job would force me to get out of the apartment.

When I mentioned the idea to my kids, they all agreed that this might be a really good thing.

I was hired the next day and soon found that being out in the community under my own terms was actually good for me. My kids noticed it right away too. My confidence began to build back up, and I was beginning to see glimpses of happiness through interacting with other humans.

II – April 2017

In late January 2016, a gentleman whom I had known for nearly twenty years, whose kids were longtime friends of Luke and Gabe, came into the bar. I approached him and when our eyes met he said, "Bonnie?"

I nodded. "Hi, Frank!"

He grabbed my forearm and said, "You look fantastic!"

Not knowing what to say, I served him and his son dinner and carried on with my job.

I began to notice him coming around the bar more frequently, either to grab a beer after work or to have dinner. Each time he came in, we would chat; when he began to express interest in taking me to coffee or on a boat ride, I shrugged him off, thinking, "This would never work... we've known each other far too long and I have way too much baggage for him to deal with."

My rejections didn't stop him from continuing to pursue me, but I always managed to find a way to tell him thanks but no.

In late April, while I was on a dinner date with another gentleman (my first date since Gabe had died), we ran into Frank. Walking into a local establishment for an after-dinner drink, Frank made eye contact with me and his face lit up with a huge smile. When he noticed a man coming in with me, I watched as his face turned from excitement to disappointment. I'd be lying if I said my heart wasn't touched by that.

Frank approached me a few minutes later and wrapped a hula hoop around me, saying, "Bonnie, teach me how to hula hoop!"

I hula hooped with him for a few minutes and then said, "Frank, I'm on a date."

His reply? "I know."

I went back to the date I was with and proceeded to watch Frank for the hour that we were there. I noticed people laughing with him, talking to him, loving on him, and I noticed that he did the same to everyone else.

I sat there thinking, "I'm on a date with the wrong guy."

As he was walking out to leave, I whispered in his ear, "I know some people who think we should date. You've only been separated for a few months. Do you think you are ready?"

He said, "Bonnie, my divorce has been coming for the last eight years. I'm ready."

With that, he walked out. I went home that night and lay in my bed, wondering what to do next.

In the morning, I sent Frank a message. It said:

"Listen to me. I've watched you at the bar. I've stalked your Facebook page. I've seen you hula hoop. After watching you last night, I spent the remainder of my evening thinking that I was on a date with the wrong man.

"I hate guns. I'm kinda liberal. I've been in a fight with God since the night I laid with my dead child. I'm kind of a mess and yet I wake up each morning with an endless amount of hope in thinking that someday, a man is going to see the mess that I am and love me anyway. There's a tiny amount of hope inside me that you might be that man.

"I don't love small. When I love, it's fierce. I know I'm far too valuable to be a rebound girl and I'm in no position to get my heart broken, so I need to know before we proceed any farther, are you ready?"

He responded simply and to the point.

"Bonnie, I think you should give me a chance. You won't regret it. I am ready. I mean it."

It was those last three words that really spoke to me; somehow I knew that he really did mean it.

Over the course of the next few weeks, we began seeing each other frequently. We spent our evenings on the boat, kayaking, going to Jordan's band concerts, talking on the phone, and just generally getting to know each other.

One night, after having a glass of wine, he walked me to my car and he kissed me.

It was electric.

And scary as hell.

For months, I had prepared a tentative plan for my future. While nothing was set in stone, I had decided that I needed to move away from this small town and find a way to start over, a reset button sort of thing. Looking back, I guess it's fair to say I just wanted to run away from all the hurt in my past, not to mention distancing myself physically from my ex-husband.

While I had contemplated the idea of finding companionship, I also knew that I couldn't settle into something that was mediocre or comfortable; if I was going to be with someone, it would have to be someone who could love me exactly as I come and who loved himself enough to have the humility to question his beliefs, prejudices and needs for comfort. A gypsy mentality, if you will—knowing that home is a feeling and not a place, change can be embraced, and understanding that comfort is supremely overrated. Even knowing that I saw these qualities in Frank, the idea that I might give my heart to someone was so frightening that I had to take a step back.

So that night, after that kiss, I went home and all I could think of was that this guy was going to get in the way of me moving, of all the plans I had for my future, because it was going to change the projection I'd already formed. All I could see in my future was me. Well, and my kids.

I didn't talk to him for three days and he finally called me up and said, "Bonnie. If you think I'm going to go away just because you got scared of a kiss, you've got another thing coming. You aren't going to get rid of me that easily."

So there he was. The man that wanted me.

Through the course of the next few months, we began spending almost all of our free time together. I felt that I owed him the respect to fill him in on the details of my failed marriage and the treatment I sustained (as well as the idea that I was really a wrecked woman), and I also gave him the entire detailed account of the night that Gabe died.

I think somehow I believed for a long time that no man was ever going to be able to love the broken woman that I really was inside. Like, there would never be a man who could handle loving me and all the baggage I come with. I really think I told him these things early on because I figured he'd run, so I may as well get that over with before I got too attached.

He didn't run.

In fact, the night that I told him about my marriage and all the hurt I'd learned to live with, he got rather pissed. I believe his exact words were, "I don't understand! I see a treasure sitting in front of me; one of the most beautiful women I've ever seen with a heart that is equally as beautiful. What kind of monster would do such things to another person, especially one as special as you are?"

The night that I told him about Gabe, he wept. He sat there and listened and looked at me, crying tears of sadness for Gabe, for me, and for my other boys.

When I was finished telling him, I was exhausted and asked him to take me home. I think at that point I figured he'd tell me the next day he didn't want to see me anymore.

Instead, I woke up the next morning when he called to let me know that he loved me more that day than he did the day before. He was learning exactly who I was and for the first time in my life, I began to feel valued by a man that I loved. I was no spare change…to Frank, I was pure gold, and so were the small pieces of copper that began to appear in his world.

I thought again about the statement Gabe made two years prior: "One day, a man is going to see every level of psycho that you are and he's going to love you anyway, and I can't wait to watch it happen…"

I mentioned earlier about the jar labeled Pennies from Heaven. Well, Frank began to find pennies too. The first one was in a tent I brought to my cousin's cabin in August. The tent hadn't been used since before Gabe died; while he was setting it up, I was filling air into the air mattress. He came running over and said, "Bonnie, put that down and come with me; I have to show you something RIGHT NOW!"

So I did.

When I stepped into the tent, I looked down and saw one penny sitting on the floor of the tent.

Gabe knew how much I loved to camp. He knew.

The second one was in his truck. We were headed to go camping in Door County for a few days and we stopped to get coffee on the way. Coming back to the truck, he looked down between the seat and the door and saw it. He just stared at it for a minute and shook his head; he had cleaned the truck top to bottom the day before and he had emptied his change pocket before he left the house that day; there was no way it had dropped out of his pocket, and based on the location of it, he wouldn't have missed it while vacuuming the truck. He looked up to the heavens with the penny in his hand and simply said, "OK, Gabe, thank you."

The third was in the shower.

While the waves of grief come less frequently than before, they still come. Though I am learning to let Frank experience the sadness with me, there are times when I still push him away; I guess the easiest way to explain it is that I don't want to pull him under with me. During one particularly difficult wave, I told him to just leave me alone. He wanted to help however he could and I wanted him to not see me in the condition that I was in.

He went home from work, not knowing what to do, and got in the shower. He looked down on the floor and next to the drain was a penny. It was like Gabe was telling him, "Don't give up. She's going to fight you every step of the way but keep trying; she'll let you back in."

And the fourth was in the parking lot at the courthouse. His divorce had been pending since April of the previous year and for reasons beyond his control, it dragged on for a longer time than it should have. In January, the morning that he went for his final divorce hearing, he pulled into the parking lot at the courthouse where there were many open spaces. He stepped out of his truck and looked down, then bent over, picked up the penny that was right next to his boot, and looked up to the sky. He knew what it meant.

And so did I.

During the time that I was dating other men, I only told my children I was going on a date. Occasionally I would ask Martha or Anne what I should wear, but I never told the kids anything about the men and I didn't introduce them to each other, either. I didn't ever want my kids to get attached or hopeful about a possible suitor for me unless I knew it was the real thing.

Jordan watched me and Frank. He spent time with us. He noticed how Frank seemed to be investing in his life, and while he never tried to tell me what to do, I know he liked him. So when I decided it was time to tell my children what was going on, I started with him.

One morning before school, after I had made Jordan his breakfast, I put the plate in front of him and simply stated, "I'm falling in love with Frank."

Jordan's eyes got really big and then filled with tears; a huge smile appeared on his face as he opened his arms to hug me and said, "Mom, that's so great!"

Ben and Martha were temporarily in Akron for baseball; Luke and Anne were living in Phoenix. I sent a group message to them that explained what was going on with Frank, and they all gave me their approval and their encouragement (well, Luke first sent a text back asking some personal questions about Frank and then stated, "Any man who's going to spend time with my mom on my watch is going to be the right man"). I think in many ways the messages that went back and forth that day gave my children some hope and peace that they likely hadn't felt in a long time. Their mom was beginning to come back.

Frank asked me, two months after we had been dating, to join him at a friend's wedding in Wyoming. I agreed to go, thinking "This is either going to make us or break us"; we had a 16-hour car ride each way and four days camping in a tent with no facilities, high in the mountains.

I'm not sure at what point it happened, but somewhere between the ten-mile hike, the 40-degree nighttime temperatures, and drinking wine from a coffee cup while he cooked us dinner over the fire, I began to acknowledge the possibility that this man might actually be my soul mate. I asked him one night early on if he believed in soul mates and he responded by saying, "Bonnie, I've just recently found mine."

As for me, well, it just began to happen…everyone who knew me and the horror story I lived through understood that I had built walls up around myself and especially my heart. I guess the best way I could say what I felt happening with Frank was that he was slowly, tenderly, and patiently chiseling away the bricks I had laid to protect myself. I was beginning to feel free, and somehow I knew that Gabe was smiling with each tap of the hammer.

One day that summer, I walked to the cemetery to visit Gabe's grave, as I do on most warm days. The walk there is pretty and it's a quiet place, and though his remains are not there, the stone reminds everyone that he existed.

Dust had settled on the stone, and for weeks, I had been retracing a message I wrote in the dust that simply said, "I love you my sunshine."

That day, as I approached the stone, I noticed that someone had wiped just that part of the stone off. I panicked. I began to hyperventilate and I started sobbing uncontrollably. I don't know if I was more upset that my note had been erased or that someone had touched something that was special between my child and me, but I was inconsolable.

I called Frank.

He stayed on the phone with me while I walked back to the apartment. Then I told him I would be OK. A few minutes later he called back and told me he was on his way. I told him not to leave work, and he yelled, "Bonnie, I'm not turning around!"

When he came into my apartment, I was watching the video we had made for Gabe's funeral. He had never seen it. He sat there and sobbed with me, crying for Gabe and for me and for my other boys.

When it was over, I told him I was going to go polish the stone, and he told me he was thinking the same thing. He drove me to the grave and we began cleaning it off, until I had another breakdown in realizing how messed up it was that I was cleaning my child's grave instead of his room.

He hugged me. He didn't try to fix me. He didn't have any "feel better" words to say. He let it be what it was: a moment of despair in the midst of a loss he knew he would never fully understand.

He helped me get into his truck. He walked back over to the stone.

He finished the job. Then, he found a purple feather and stuck it in the ground next to the grave.

It was on that day that I knew something extraordinary was happening between Frank, myself, and Gabe, and never for a moment have I thought differently since then.

Gabe is on the other side, but he is watching, and he likes what he sees.

Around the same time as my relationship with Frank was beginning, a year and a half after Gabe had died, my children began to see other blessings.

Ben had been called up to AAA with his team and was throwing so well that he was part of a trade with another team in July of that year (2016). Two weeks after that trade, I was sleeping when my phone rang at midnight. During the playing season, my communication with Ben is fairly limited; while I do go see him at least a couple of times each summer, he really only calls me when either a) he needs to hear my voice, or b) he has news about baseball. Other than that, we text briefly and send snap chats to each other just to let the other know we're all right.

So when the phone rang at midnight, I got scared for a minute that something was wrong. After assuring me that everything was fine, he told me that if I didn't have anything to do the next day, I might want to go to Fenway Park since he'd be there with his team.

And just like that, my boy's dream had come true.

I woke up Jordan and we packed a bag and drove to Chicago, where we bought two plane tickets and arrived in Boston at 6:00 the next morning.

Ben didn't get to pitch that night or the next, while I was there, and though he was optioned down to AAA again for ten days, he was called back up in late August and made his debut at Yankee Stadium a few nights later.

I didn't see his debut because I had run out of money after traveling to Boston, New York and Seattle in an attempt to see it, but the day of the game I recall talking to him and telling him that even though he wouldn't see my face, I was most definitely going to be there with him, and so was Gabe.

He said, "Oh, I know."

Ben bought Luke a plane ticket to his debut game, yearning to have him see how all those hours spent practicing with him had come to fruition. With over 40,000 fans watching the game, a foul ball hit by a player while Ben was pitching, which could have wound up in any one of those fans' palms, landed right in Luke's hand. Many might call that coincidence, but we know better... Gabe *was* there and now we all have proof.

Tell me Gabe isn't orchestrating our lives.

Luke and Anne, living in Phoenix mainly because Luke felt he needed to be closer to Ben, were not enjoying big-city living, and they missed the seasons that the Midwest offers. One day, completely out of the blue, Luke received an offer from his former college assistant coach, who was now the head coach at the same college, to be the pitching coach. Luke hadn't ever thought about the idea of coaching and was confused for quite some time about whether he should take the job, but after much prayerful consideration, decided that he couldn't pass up the opportunity to work with young people in that capacity. He and Anne moved back to Grand Rapids last August and have never once regretted their decision.

Tell me Gabe isn't laying the groundwork for our futures.

Jordan never did well in school; he had a hard time learning the way most teachers thought he should and because of that, got by with mostly average to below average grades, hating nearly every class (with the exception of science, band and tech ed). His behavior and general attitude about school caused him to be more of a headache for much of the high school staff. Last May, he was invited to a scholarship night and was presented with $3,500 in scholarships to help him pay for his schooling at a tech school in Phoenix. He was humbled at the support he was shown that night, and I can report that at this moment he has a 4.0 GPA, and appears to be enjoying the way they are schooling him. While he doesn't intend to stay in Phoenix, it has been wonderful watching him finally flourish at something he loves, which is exactly the same "Fuck what everyone wants you to do… do what YOU want" message that Gabe had been trying to tell him for years, as his confusion and dread of going to a four-year school would cause him anxiety.

Tell me Gabe isn't saying, "See…I told you so… You got this, brother!"

People frequently ask me, "How are you, Bonnie?"

I usually have to pause for a moment to decide if I need to state the "qualifier"…explaining before I respond that I wish my child was still here.

For reasons I can't really explain, I find it to be dishonoring to Gabe if I say that I'm actually doing well. Under the circumstances, I feel like I *am* doing well. Would I likely be doing much better if Gabe were here? Absolutely. Each time I am asked, I have to evaluate the condition of the heart of the asker so that I know how much I need to say.

One day, I ran into one of Gabe's close friends, Tommy. He came up behind me and gave me a huge hug and said, "Bonnie, how are you doing?"

I looked at him and honestly answered, "Oh Tommy, I'm getting a little better every day."

He smiled and then said, "I'm so proud of you."

Be still my heart.

III - May 2017

Last month, Frank made a phone call to Ben, to Luke and to Jordan. He already knew Gabe's response to the question he would ask each of them.

When he explained that he was calling to get permission to ask for their mom's hand in marriage, each one, without any hesitation, said (I paraphrase), "Oh, hell yes."

Those boys and their girls have fallen madly in love with Frank, not because of who he is as a man or a human, but because of the way he loves me. They are seeing, for the first time, their mom being respected and honored and loved, and it fills them with satisfaction. The confusion in their heads is no more.

Frank asked me at three o'clock in the morning, after I worked a closing shift, when he grunted and then told me he couldn't wait a minute longer. "Will you be my wife?"

I said yes and he slipped a ring on my finger.

This entire book could be summed up in the little story I shared with my friends:

"Once upon a time, there was a girl. Her story had just enough dark pages to keep her thinking she was meant to be alone.

"Once upon a time there was a boy. He wasn't scared of anything. He read her story and gently took her hand and said, 'Come with me; I'm going to show you what love looks like.'

"So she went. And she learned that even though he couldn't erase the dark pages, he was really good at holding a flashlight so that she could see more clearly. She began to have new pages, filled with smiles and laughter and hope.

"One day that boy asked the girl to be his wife. She said yes."

Made in the USA
Lexington, KY
17 July 2017